The Great I Am

'I am the LORD your God, who brought you out of Egypt, out of the land of slavery.'
Exodus 20:2

Selwyn Hughes & Philip Greenslade
Revised and updated by Mick Brooks
FURTHER STUDY: IAN SEWTER

© CWR 2013. Dated text previously published as *Every Day with Jesus: The Great Escape* (July/August 2001) by CWR. This edition revised and updated for 2013 by Mick Brooks.

CWR, Waverley Abbey House, Waverley Lane, Farnham, Surrey GU9 8EP, UK
Tel: 01252 784700 Email: mail@cwr.org.uk
Registered Charity No. 294387. Registered Limited Company No. 1990308.

Unless otherwise stated, all Scripture quotations are from the Holy Bible, New International Version. © International Bible Society.
Cover image: getty/Brand X/Morey Milbradt
Quiet Time image: Simon Ray@CWR
Printed in England by Linney Print

MIX
Paper from
responsible sources
FSC® C015900
www.fsc.org

CWR

A word of introduction ...

'Travelogs' consume a vast amount of shelf space in bookshops and are now the focus of many online blogs. It's become quite the thing to post on the internet, for all to see, your travel photos and details of adventures, close shaves and cross-cultural miscommunications. However, travelogs are not a new phenomenon.

Perhaps no travelog has been read and retold in books, plays and movies more than that in the book of Exodus. The tale of the journey of the children of Israel from Egypt to Canaan is perhaps the greatest escape story ever – the movement of an entire people from slavery to freedom. It is a gripping narrative, beginning with Joseph and ending with the awesome image of God's glory filling the tabernacle.

Although it's not been possible to cover in one issue everything that happens in Exodus, Selwyn has been able to highlight many of the major events and revelations, reminding us that the God of Exodus is the same today. He still hears the cry of His people, still saves, still guides and is present with us each day on our own journeys to the promised new creation.

The amazing book of Exodus is almost certainly the 'ultimate summer read' – containing adventure, biography, history, geography and up-close accounts of blessing and tragedy – the whole spectrum of human experience can be found here! Over the next two months, I hope that you, like the characters in this book, will discover 'The Great I Am', who brings you out of 'slavery' and into the joy of His freedom.

Mick Brooks, Consulting Editor

Free small-group resources to accompany this issue can be found at www.cwr.org.uk/extra. The *EDWJ* Facebook community is growing! To join the conversation visit www.facebook.com/edwjpage

The benchmark of power

FOR READING & MEDITATION - EXODUS 1:1-5

'The descendants of Jacob numbered seventy in all;
Joseph was already in Egypt.' (v.5)

Today we begin a devotional study of the second book in the Old Testament – Exodus. This book is of special importance because the people who feature in its story are those to whom the whole of the Old Testament was given. The title 'Exodus' reflects 'The Great Escape' of the Israelites from slavery in Egypt, a miracle of deliverance by God, 'The Great I Am'. This deliverance became the benchmark of God's power, displaying His character and presence.

The book opens by linking us immediately with the story of Joseph, told in Genesis, in order to explain why the sons of Jacob had come to live in Egypt. Jacob, having discovered that his son Joseph was alive, left the land of Canaan and moved his family to Egypt to be with him, and there he finally ended his days. Within the protective 'womb' of Egypt the seventy-strong family of Jacob rapidly multiplied until they became a huge presence in the land. At this point in time a new king arises – a king who neither remembers Joseph's involvement in the nation nor has any regard for his descendants. The new king, fearing that in the event of war the Israelites might prove an internal threat, decides to make them slaves.

How did the Almighty God, the One who cares, guides, delivers, and opposes oppression, respond to this? He plans their freedom, and the narrative of how that freedom was brought about is the theme of this book. God, we should understand, does not want to control people but to set them free. However, true freedom, as Abraham Lincoln put it, 'is not the right to do what we want but the power to do what we ought'. We are never truly free until we submit to the purposes of God.

FURTHER STUDY

Gen. 15:12-16;
Eph. 1:3-14;
Rev. 13:8

1. When did God plan the Israelites' freedom?

2. When did God plan our freedom?

O Father, help me not only understand but enter into the joy of this blessed paradox, namely that the more yielded I am to Your purposes the more my soul is set free. I want to be Your willing servant for ever. Amen.

Waiting for deliverance

FOR READING & MEDITATION - EXODUS 1:6-14

'... in all their hard labour the Egyptians used them ruthlessly.' (v.14)

Yesterday we ended with the thought that we are never truly free until we submit to the purposes of God. The issue for the Israelites was to whom they should give their allegiance. To an earthly power or a heavenly one? That same challenge faces us too.

Clearly, the Pharaoh who arose after Joseph had died repudiated the favourable relationship which Joseph had established between the Israelites and the Egyptian authorities. The rapid growth of the Israelites (v.7), we should understand, was in line with the command of God recorded in Genesis 1:28: 'Be fruitful and increase in number.' The new king's anxiety at the increase of the Israelites brings him into direct conflict with the Creator. Later, as we shall see from the plagues that were to devastate Egypt, God demonstrates in the face of rebellion His power over the forces of creation.

FURTHER STUDY

Acts 16:16-40;
Heb. 4:14-16

1. Why did God not deliver Paul from the mob?

2. How do we draw upon grace?

It's strange to me that God does not immediately set about delivering His people, and the long period the Israelites have to wait before being finally set free seems to militate against all that Scripture has to say about a concerned and caring God. Which of us hasn't cried out to God, 'Lord, if You love me why don't You deliver me from these difficult and distressing circumstances?' Perhaps you are in that situation right now. If so, let this thought sustain you: God does not desert the bewildered individuals who feel that He has forgotten to be gracious and that their prayers are going unheeded. Remember, timing is everything with God. The day of deliverance will come. Until then He supplies the grace which, if drawn upon, is more than a match for anything.

Lord Jesus Christ, You who knew what it was to cry, 'May this cup be taken from me,' help me also to say, as You did, 'Yet not as I will, but as you will.' For Your own dear name's sake. Amen.

'Creative disobedience'

FOR READING & MEDITATION – EXODUS 1:15-22

'The midwives, however, feared God and did not do what the king of Egypt had told them to do ...' (v.17)

One of the great truths of Scripture – and one we must hold on to in these days when there is so much resistance against the things of God – is this: His purposes are never blocked by manmade barriers. Ultimately God will bring His plans to fruition despite every form of resistance, often by utilising the very opposition of men – and even their anger! The psalmist understood this for he wrote, 'Surely the wrath of man shall praise you ...' (Psa. 76:10, NKJV).

So it is here. Not for the first or last time the story hinges on the heroic courage and enterprise of faithful women. These intrepid heroines of faith outwit the king of Egypt. The Hebrew midwives practised 'passive resistance' or, as someone has put it, 'creative disobedience'. As God's people, it needs to be said, we are under no obligation to cooperate with the unjust or violent, be they husbands, bosses or rulers! These midwives were fearless before men because, as our text for today tells us, they 'feared God'. 'Fear God,' it has been said, 'and you will fear nothing else.'

We can take comfort from two things here: one is the fact that, I believe, nothing can happen to us that cannot, in turn, bless us and be turned to our good. Everything that happens to God's people has first to pass through His hands, as we see from the opening chapters of Job. Second, small acts of courage have a big impact on the world. It was C.S. Lewis who commented that cowardice and Christ do not fit together. Wherever you are today and whatever you do, stand up and be counted if that is what is needed. Have the courage of your convictions and be assured of this: it can and will make a difference to the big picture of what God is achieving on the earth!

FURTHER STUDY

Dan. 1:1-17;
Rom. 1:16-17

1. How did Daniel practise creative disobedience?

2. What was Paul's conviction?

O Father, let me grasp these two simple but sublime truths, namely that nothing can ever happen to me without Your permission, and that my stand for truth really does make a difference. I am so thankful. In Jesus' name. Amen.

Providential preservation

FOR READING & MEDITATION - EXODUS 2:1-10

'Then she placed the child in [a papyrus basket] and put it among the reeds along the bank of the Nile.' (v.3)

The more we explore Exodus the more vulnerable God appears to be in risking His plans in fallible human hands. His saving purposes for the future hang on the slender thread of what happens to the children of Israel and now, even more, are focused in the fate of this one child! And notice again how the action is in debt to quick-witted and brave women – in this case Moses' mother and sister. Even Pharaoh's daughter defies her father's murderous decree! These woman are pro-life in a culture of death. They vote for tenderness in a climate of violence, and God is with them. Their 'motherly' instincts, so crucial to the story, are matched by God's parental attitude.

FURTHER STUDY

Matt. 2:7-23;
Acts 9:17-25

1. How was Moses' early life a type of Christ's?

2. How might we be involved in our own deliverance?

Like Noah, Moses is threatened with 'drowning' (1:22), is entrusted to his 'ark' (the Hebrew word translated 'papyrus basket' in 2:3 is also used of Noah's ark), and is drawn from the waters of death (2:5). The threat hanging over all the 'sons of Israel' (1:1ff.), then all the male sons (1:16), is now concentrated in one son who will himself eventually lead Israel to freedom as the 'firstborn son of God' (4:22–24).

Reflect too on the delicious ironies of God's working. Moses is saved by a member of Pharaoh's own family. As a 'prince of Egypt' he is educated in the skills of diplomacy and leadership – an all-expenses-paid education courtesy of the very regime God will use him to undermine! God indeed has the last word against arrogant, God-defying power and oppression. Notice too that in this section there is no direct mention of God at all! Often He works unobtrusively, using fragile human channels, but He is never in the end successfully thwarted! Can anything be more encouraging and comforting?

O God, open my eyes to see that nothing can successfully work against Your purposes. Some may try to pit their weight and wits against You, but they can never win. I am so grateful that You are on my side and that I am on Yours. Amen.

Partners in God's purpose

FOR READING & MEDITATION – EXODUS 2:11-22

'An Egyptian rescued us from the shepherds. He even drew water for us and watered the flock.' (v.19)

How mixed are our motives and actions. Here we see Moses commendably concerned with justice, first by intervening when he witnessed one of his fellow countrymen being beaten, and later by coming to the aid of the Midianite girls. But to act out of a sense of personal grievance or even 'righteous anger' does not guarantee that God's purpose is being served. In a sense, Moses anticipates what God will do: he sees how God's people are being oppressed and strikes hard against the enemy (the same word is later used of God's actions against Egypt). The problem was that by taking matters into his own hands he was pre-empting God's initiative. God would deal with the Egyptians in His time and in His way. Moses' behaviour during this period of his life seems to prefigure that of the later Israelites who one moment were obedient, the next moment self-willed. Did he, perhaps, foresee the wilderness wanderings and the Exile when he cried, 'I have become an alien in a foreign land' (v.22)? We should keep in mind that however much we wish to help people it is always wise to discover God's timing and whether or not what we want to do is in harmony with His ways.

FURTHER STUDY

Luke 22:31-34, 54-62;
John 21:15-19

1. Why did Peter deny Christ?

2. How did Jesus view Peter's imperfections?

Biblical heroes such as Moses come 'warts and all'. Scripture never attempts to cover up the character flaws of the people whose lives are recorded on its pages. We are shown all sides of their character. What does that say to us? It says that God does not wait until we are perfect before He uses us. He does not delight in our imperfections, of course, but He does not disregard us because of them either. God can, does and *will* transform the most unlikely people into partners in His purpose.

O Father, I long to always be at my best for You, but I am heartened by the fact that You will not toss me on the scrap heap because of my flaws. Fill me with Yourself so that I will be all You want me to be. In Jesus' name. Amen.

The turning point

FOR READING & MEDITATION - EXODUS 2:23-25

'The Israelites groaned in their slavery ... and their cry for help because of their slavery went up to God.' (v.23)

Unbeknown to the Israelites, through the birth and protection of Moses, God has already taken the first step towards freeing His people. Meanwhile, as today's reading tells us, a 'long period' elapses, during which we may wonder what is happening in Egypt. Has God forgotten His people's plight? His seeming absence and inactivity during this time raises the tension in the story. God, it seems, becomes overtly involved only when 'the king of Egypt died'. However, we must not mistake His apparent absence for indifference. The narrative shows Him working unobtrusively and steadily through human agents. We need to learn, as someone has said, that 'God moves in long orbits, out of sight and sound, but He always arrives in His own time'.

FURTHER STUDY

Psa. 42:1-11; 43:1-5

1. What did the psalmist feel?

2. What did the psalmist decide?

Now comes the turning point in the book and, indeed, in the whole story. 'The Israelites groaned ... and ... *God heard their groaning*' (vv.23-24, my emphasis). Continually we need to remind ourselves that *God is a listening God.* He most definitely hears the groans of His people who cry out to Him for help. The Israelites' cry is not only a shriek of pain but also a legal protest against injustice. And God hears! He sides with a people who refuse to accept injustice and will respond to their cries with compassion and concern. If the Israelites could have seen the movements in heaven they would have known that help was on the way – not in their time, but in God's time.

Sir Winston Churchill once addressed a graduation ceremony at a prestigious university and said with great emphasis, 'Never give up, never, never give up, never, never, never give up!' That is God's message to you today. Don't give up.

My Father and my God, thank You for this empowering word. In response to the message I have received from You today I will hold on to the task You have given me. I will go on and not give up. In Jesus' name. Amen.

CWR Ministry Events

TE	EVENT	PLACE	PRESENTER(S)
ul	Preaching Evangelistically	Waverley Abbey House	Andy Peck
Jul	Women's Summer Weekend	Pilgrim Hall	Lynn Penson
2 Jul	Seniors' Summer Holiday	PH	Derek & Margaret Martin
ul	Help! I Want to Understand the Bible	WAH	Andy Peck and Lynette Brooks
ul	Hearing the Voice of God	WAH	Andy Peck
Jul	Open Day/Commissioning Service	PH	
Jul	Mentoring Others	WAH	Peter Jackson
Jul	Insight into Forgiveness	WAH	Mary Higginson
2 Aug	Family Summer Holiday	PH	Jon & Sarah Stannard
Aug	Overcoming the Giants - Insight into Anxiety	WAH	Chris Ledger
16 Aug	Introduction to Biblical Care and Counselling	WAH	Angie Coombes and Team
Aug	Study Skills	WAH	Mary Higginson and Kathy Overton
-31 Aug	Developing an Integrative Approach to Counselling	WAH	Mary Higginson
Aug	Handling the Pressure	WAH	Beverley Shepherd

ease also pray for students and tutors on our ongoing **BA in Counselling** ogramme at Waverley and Pilgrim Hall and our **Certificate and Diploma Christian Counselling** and **MA in Integrative Psychotherapy** held at ndon School of Theology.

For further details and a full list of CWR's courses, phone +44 (0)1252 784719, or visit the CWR website at **www.cwr.org.uk**

Covenant love

FOR READING & MEDITATION - EXODUS 2:23-25

'God heard their groaning and he remembered his covenant with Abraham, with Isaac and with Jacob.' (v.24)

So important are these three moving verses which tell us that God hears and responds to the groaning of His oppressed people, that we shall spend another day considering them. One statement made in these verses shows us that the reaction in the divine heart is not just a passing emotional response but one that is very profound: 'God ... remembered his covenant ...' Divine love is not only a *compassionate* love but a *covenant* love. 'Covenant' adds steel and depth to the notion of God's love, which is later described as 'steadfast' or 'enduring'. God's compassion evokes within Him the memory of His covenant promises to the patriarchs – made first to Abraham, and repeated to Isaac and Jacob – that Abraham's descendants would be the means of bringing blessing and salvation to all the nations of the earth.

FURTHER STUDY

Psa. 136:1-26;
Isa. 49:8-16;
James 2:15-16

1. What is the difference between compassion and covenant love?

2. Why can God never forget us?

Throughout the Scriptures we are told that our salvation depends on God *remembering* His covenant promises, just as it does on Him forgetting the sins He forgives! God's memory is our hope! He will not forget you or His covenant promises which include you. The Creator's love for His people is a *listening and a loyal love*. God 'heard', not because He was deaf before but in the sense of actively responding. God 'remembered', not as if He had suffered from amnesia but in the sense that He acted to implement His previous commitments. God 'looked', not merely in the sense of noticing but in being moved to sympathy. God 'knew', not merely as a matter of information but in being concerned, becoming involved and entering into the experience of those who were suffering. A God as loving and loyal as this deserves a loving and loyal response.

O God my Father, how thankful I am that Your love is not just a compassionate love but a covenant love. You are committed to me through an agreement that will never be nullified. My gratitude knows no bounds. Amen.

FOR READING & MEDITATION – EXODUS 3:1-5
'... God called to him from within the bush, "Moses! Moses!"' (v.4)

We come now to an exciting and pivotal moment in the exodus story – the moment when God makes Himself known to Moses. No doubt Moses had seen other desert bushes spontaneously ignite and then burn out. But as he walks slowly ahead of his flock he becomes curious because the bush is not consumed. This burning bush was a great attention-getter. Yet even in unexceptional circumstances the natural world is a 'theatre of God's glory' and can become a means of grace and joy to us. Moses, attracted by the sight and personally addressed by a voice calling to him, concedes he is on holy ground! He has a strong sense of reverence and awe. Moses took off his shoes – we would probably react by taking off our coats!

This incident occurred at the foot of Horeb 'the mountain of God' (v.1). God did not reveal Himself there because Horeb was a special mountain; it became special because God revealed Himself there! Any 'bush' can become the place where we encounter God – be it a park bench, an attic or even a crowded commuter train.

God stirred up Moses' curiosity in order to draw him to a place where He could make Himself known. And He will do the same for you. In some way He will get your attention, and when He does you will find yourself catching a new glimpse of Him, and realising that His Word is making a deeper impression on you than it has done before. But remember, this happens not to enable you to stockpile spiritual experiences. God's purpose is to engage you as a partner in His long-term plans to bring blessing to others and salvation to this world.

FURTHER STUDY

Acts 3:1-4:4

1. What got the people's attention?

2. What was the result?

O Father, forgive me if I am so preoccupied with trivial things that You find it necessary to crash into my life with an attention-getter. However, if You need to then help me be willing to carry out everything You intend me to do. Amen.

For more on dramatic encounters with God, see *God Unannounced*, compiled by Andy Peck, which contains stories of revival from around the world. Available from CWR.

Whatever you need

FOR READING & MEDITATION - EXODUS 3:6-14

'God said to Moses, 'I AM WHO I AM.'' (v.14)

Having gained Moses' attention, God reminds him of the relationship He established with Abraham, Isaac and Jacob. He then reveals His determination to become involved with the suffering of His people and to rescue them. All this is music to Moses' ears until he hears the words, 'So now, go. I am sending you to Pharaoh ...' (v.10). Standing before a blazing fire, Moses suddenly gets cold feet! God's commission sounded like 'mission impossible'.

By responding with the question 'Who am I?' Moses became the first in a long line of reluctant biblical heroes. His reaction is understandable, of course; having heard what God had pledged to do, Moses might well have assumed that He did not need his help! Immediately God reassures Moses that His presence will be with him, but that he will know this fully only in retrospect when he arrives with the freed slaves at this very mountain to worship Him! God gives no guarantees about the future that do not call for faith.

FURTHER STUDY

Judg. 6:1-16,27

1. What was Gideon's response to God's call?

2. What was God's response to Gideon's doubts?

Moses' initial 'Who am I?' – a sign of his reluctance and self-doubt – is swallowed up in a bigger question: 'Who are You?' 'What is Your name?' In other words, 'Who is authorising me to do this?' God's reply – a virtually untranslatable version of the verb 'to be' – has become the source of much theological speculation. But in this context the accent is less on God's self-sufficiency – true as that is – than on His desire to be intimately involved with His people: 'I will be what I will be.' The God we worship is self-sufficient, but He delights in sharing with His people from His great sufficiency. Never forget, He is the God 'who is able to do immeasurably more than all we ask or imagine' (Eph. 3:20).

O God, let the full weight of this wonderful word cover my heart like a blanket. I would walk in its warmth not only today but every day. You are my never-failing supply. I am deeply, deeply grateful. Amen.

Finding out who God is

'And I have promised to bring you up out of your misery in Egypt ...'
(v.17)

How wonderful that the Almighty God is willing to enter into dialogue with Moses and in that conversation reveal so much about Himself and His nature. As indicated later in Exodus (6:3), there is more to this conversation than the revelation of an entirely new name. God had always been Yahweh, even to the patriarchs (v.15). But He had not made Himself known in His *full* capacity as Yahweh until now.

Moses is commanded to go in the authority of God's full name: 'The LORD [Yahweh], the God of your fathers ... has sent me to you' (v.15). But the elusive nature of the name – 'I AM WHO I AM' or 'I will be what I will be' – means, in the writer Terence Fretheim's words, that only 'Israel's own experience with God in history will confirm the meaning of this name'. The God who has proved Himself faithful in keeping His promises to the fathers, who watches over His people and sees what is happening to them now in Egypt, will in the future bring them up out of the land of Egypt into a well provided land.

FURTHER STUDY

Matt. 1:18-25;
Acts 4:5-12

1. What is special about Christ's names?

2. What did Peter explain?

Like Moses and the people of Israel, we too travel a journey and trust this same God in order to find out who He really is. It is one thing to have our theory about God all nicely packaged and in biblical order; it is another to walk by faith into the future and put our full confidence in Him. We must not be like the little boy who, after a ride on a friend's donkey, said, 'I didn't want to tire the donkey out so I didn't put my whole weight down!' Søren Kierkegaard, the Danish philosopher, is reported to have said, 'Life can be understood backwards, but it has to be lived forwards.' Blessed are they who 'live life forwards', believing that God will be all He has said He will be.

My Father and my God, as I look back over my life I see the tracks of Your footsteps alongside mine. I cannot see into the future but You can. And I know that You will be then all You have been to me in the past. Amen.

Excuses! Excuses!

FOR READING & MEDITATION - EXODUS 4:1-9

'Moses answered, "What if they do not believe me
or listen to me ...?"' (v.1)

Moses, understandably, is wary of being drawn into the 'mission impossible' God has in mind for him, so he delves deep into his reserve of excuses. 'What if they do not believe me?' he says. This, of course, is a very human reaction, and you may well have responded to a call from God in a similar way. The attitude 'What if …?' is a stock weapon in our armoury of self-defence mechanisms. 'What if I discipline my children and they go off me?' 'What if I pray and get no answer?' 'What if I respond to God's call and I run out of money?' 'What if …?' so often paralyses us and prevents us following hard after God.

FURTHER STUDY

Esth. 3:13-4:17

1. What excuses did Esther make?

2. How were her excuses overcome?

But God will not let Moses off the hook and now makes obedience childishly simple. 'What is that in your hand?' He asks him (v.2). Moses doesn't need a degree in Egyptian Logic to answer that; he can't avoid the question. 'A staff,' he replies. 'Throw it on the ground,' God tells him. What follows is the first of three signs which will confirm Moses' authority. Moses' action of taking the staff-turned-snake by the tail indicates the triumph of God's power over Egypt since the snake was a symbol of Egyptian royal authority, as seen in the Pharaoh's cobra-like headdress.

Our journey in the Christian life may well begin with God seeking to overcome our defences by asking us this simple question, 'What is it you *can* do?' Do what is in your heart and in your hand to do! Write that letter, make that phone call, offer that apology, take up the thing you know should be done. Ask yourself now, 'What simple action do I need to take in obedience to God that will trigger a greater demonstration of His presence?' You do the possible; God will do the impossible. It's often as simple as that.

O God, forgive me for the excuses I hide behind whenever You seek to prod me to greater effectiveness in Your kingdom. I surrender them all to You now. Speak Lord, Your servant is listening. Amen.

Still more excuses!

FOR READING & MEDITATION - EXODUS 4:10-17

'Moses said to the Lord, "O Lord, I have never been eloquent ..."'
(v.10)

Moses is given another sign to show that God is with him. Like the first sign, the second also signifies God's power over natural forces, in this case over disease. A third sign, too, is promised, one that anticipates the first plague by showing God's power over the River Nile – the essential life-force sustaining Egypt.

Yet not even the promise of signs is enough to deter Moses from his excuses; he now claims lack of eloquence! Did he feel his Egyptian was a bit rusty after so long in the desert or that shepherds' talk was not the best preparation for such high diplomacy? Whatever the reason, it would appear that God's conversation with him had made no difference whatsoever, and that he thought if only he had employed a spin doctor he could have talked God out of sending him at all! But nothing can divert the determination of the Creator God, who can help with both speech and message. Can anything be fairer than that?

Finally Moses stops all his excuses and asks desperately for God to find someone else to do the job (v.13)! In response God makes Aaron Moses' spokesman. It is clear that God's will does not depend on human eloquence; any mouthpiece (remember the story of Balaam's donkey in Numbers 22?) – like any bush – will do! This is not to disparage human talents, of course; Moses obviously had leadership gifts. But we make the point again: God does not need a perfect vehicle to accomplish His tasks. He can overcome all our weaknesses provided we allow Him to. Always remember that, given our consent and obedience, God can turn ineffectiveness to effectiveness, paralysis to power, and inadequacy to sufficiency.

FURTHER STUDY

Jer. 1:1-19

1. What was Jeremiah's excuse?

2. What was God's response?

Once again I pray heavenly Father that You will expose my excuses and rationalisations. Help me to offer myself for service in a new way. I ask this in Jesus' name. Amen.

Israel – 'God's son'

FOR READING & MEDITATION – EXODUS 4:18-31

'Let my son go, so that he may worship me.' (v.23)

A remarkable phrase appears in the section we have read today. Moses is instructed to declare to Pharaoh that Israel is God's firstborn son and must be allowed to go. This statement is crucial for the unfolding of the rest of the biblical story. Connected to this statement is the death of the firstborn in Egypt (v.23b) and the later consecration of every Israelite's firstborn to God.

This fatherly image of God is not incompatible with the seemingly tougher picture of a sovereign God who will harden Pharaoh's heart in order to further His purposes.

FURTHER STUDY

John 1:1-13;
Rom. 8:29;
Gal. 3:26-4:7

1. How do we become a son of God?

2. What is a son of God to become?

We will explore more about this later, but suffice it to say here that its mention at this point in the book reminds us that the exodus story all along is meant to demonstrate the absolute control of God not only over the weakness and reluctance of His servants but also over the rebellion and opposition of earthly rulers, including powerful despots such as Pharaoh. What might seem to be unfair to Pharaoh is being done in the cause of justice and to unseat a cruel and viciously unjust tyrant!

We need sharp reminders that God is not a meek and passive deity, as is shown by the strange incident in which He threatens Moses' life (v.24). Moses had evidently neglected to circumcise his son – the key sign of the covenant. God would not allow anything associated with His plans for redemption to be ignored. So much is at stake that Moses, because of his forgetfulness, comes within an inch of his life. This incident anticipates later events which show that only the shedding of blood is effective in dealing with sin. Not for the first time Moses is saved by a woman's wit and wisdom.

Father, I see how much the shedding of blood means to You, for it is through the shed blood of Jesus that I am saved. Help me to understand more deeply the truth that without the shedding of blood there is no remission for sin. Amen.

The bread of life, with love ...

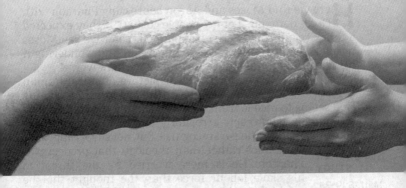

... from you, to Christians in need, both at home and overseas, who seek – like you – the sustenance of biblically-based guidance, teaching and resources.

In Galilee, Jesus told the crowd of over 4,000 to sit down,

'Then he took the seven loaves and the fish, and when he had given thanks, he broke them and gave them to the disciples, and they in turn to the people. They all ate and were satisfied' (Matt. 15:36-37).

With your help, the ministry of CWR can feed the faith of many.

Please fill in the 'Gift to CWR' section on the order form at the back of this publication, completing the Gift Aid declaration if appropriate.

Pharaoh versus God

FOR READING & MEDITATION - EXODUS 5:1-21

'Pharaoh said, "Who is the Lᴏʀᴅ, that I should obey him and let Israel go?"' (v.2)

Here we find Moses and Aaron addressing Pharaoh with God's demand, 'Let my people go' (v.1). If they expected a quick result they were disappointed. Later we see Moses perplexed at the run of events (vv.22–23) and wondering if his confrontational stance has made matters worse!

In this chapter we have a clear picture of sinful human stubbornness clashing with the divine purposes. For a while God seems to recede from the story leaving the centre stage to Pharaoh, who reacts arrogantly and dismissively to the claims of a God he doesn't recognise. But, not surprisingly, it's economics rather than theology that preoccupies Pharaoh. He is more worried by the threat to his slave labour force than the thought that he might be going against the will of the Creator of the universe (v.5). In a style characteristic of totalitarian dictators he stereotypes the people he is oppressing as 'lazy' and acts to intensify their misery by making their work impossibly arduous. This disdain for Moses and for Moses' God shows that the real conflict in the exodus story is not between Israel and Egypt or Moses and Egypt, but between *God and Pharaoh*. Pharaoh was regarded as a godlike figure whose semi-divine status was backed by the false gods of Egypt (see 12:12).

FURTHER STUDY

Matt. 6:19-34;
Col. 3:1-6

1. What did Jesus explain?

2. Why might Christians be guilty of idolatry?

Pharaoh forces the issue: 'Don't worship your God,' he instructs. 'Work for me!' Yet he asks the right question: 'Who is the Lᴏʀᴅ, that I should obey him?' Who indeed! This is the issue at the heart of the thrilling story of Exodus: who will Israel serve – Pharaoh or God? Perhaps we ought to pause here and ask ourselves: Who do we really serve? God or an idolatrous economic system? Who is our real Lord and Master?

Father, something is being burned into my consciousness - the fact that I cannot serve two masters. I renounce all other claims on my soul and offer it to You alone. You are my Master and my Lord. I bow to Your commands. Amen.

God's mighty hand

FOR READING & MEDITATION - EXODUS 5:22-6:27

'Moreover, I have heard the groaning of the Israelites ...
and I have remembered my covenant.' (6:5)

In this section we see Moses evidently smarting with humiliation, complaining to God that his mission has made matters worse for Israel. But God's vision, it seems, is larger than Moses' temporary embarrassment. In chapter 6 God's covenant purposes are again outlined in detail. Once more God reminds Moses of His past commitments in making promises to the patriarchs (v.3ff), and He pledges to renew that covenant with the current generation of Jacob's sons by bringing them into the long-promised land (v.8). In this way, this present generation will know the full significance of Yahweh's name – as previous generations had not.

What is particularly remarkable here is that the Israelites were so discouraged and embittered that they could not hear the good news when it was given to them. How often in counselling and pastoral care do we find people in this same situation. Because they feel so dejected and resentful they cannot even see the escape route God offers them from their troubles. That is why those involved in counselling and pastoral care often need to stay with people – they need to give them a glimpse of hope so that the good news can take root in their hearts.

Faced by this further unexpected setback, Moses resurrects his old argument about being inadequate for the task. The truncated genealogy that follows is perhaps meant to establish Aaron's credentials as Moses' mouthpiece. Whatever the reason for its inclusion, it shows us once again how determined God is to bring His people to freedom and how wonderfully willing He is to use fragile and complex human agents to do so!

FURTHER STUDY

Deut. 7:6-9;
1 Pet. 5:1-7

1. Why did God choose the Israelites?

2. How should we respond to God's mighty hand?

O gracious Father, grant that no matter what discouragements or disappointments I might face I will never turn a deaf ear when You tell me the way You want me to go. I rest in Your love and compassion. In Jesus' name. Amen.

'Like God'

FOR READING & MEDITATION - EXODUS 6:28-7:13

'See, I have made you like God to Pharaoh, and your brother Aaron
will be your prophet.' (7:1)

What an astonishing statement God makes to Moses when the latter, still preoccupied with his shortcomings as a persuasive advocate, is given the astounding reassurance that he has been made 'like God' to Pharaoh and that Aaron is his prophet. Extraordinary as this is in the context, it can be seen as an extension of the normal human vocation to be the image-bearer of God. After all, the purpose of our creation as human beings is to represent God's authority and character on earth. Israel was called to model humanity as God, from the very beginning, had intended it to be.

FURTHER STUDY

Eph. 4:32-5:2;
1 John 4:7-21

1. How can we be like God?

2. When are we not like God?

When Aaron's staff turned into a snake and swallowed up the Egyptians' staffs and snakes it was a vivid sign of the one Creator's supremacy over all rivals, devaluing the Egyptian kings whose royal dress was decorated with the insignia of a writhing serpent. We must never forget that God's intention is to overcome chaos and restore the order that was established at creation. He has called us by our very creation, which has been renewed through redemption, to stand on our feet and stand up to ungodliness wherever we find it. For all our own complicity in sin, for all our own inadequacy, we are, we must remember, God's people. Our commission is to overcome with good and to lay claim to every area of God's world as rightfully His. Being 'like God' does not mean that we are taken up into the Godhead and given complete knowledge; rather, it is a matter of acting as God would act within the limitations of our humanity.

How different the Church would be if we were more Godlike in our actions and behaviour. We would not need to pray for revival; we would find ourselves engulfed by it.

Father, forgive us that though we have been made in Your image we so seldom reflect that image. We are broken image-bearers reflecting only a little of Your light. Forgive us and restore us. In Jesus' name. Amen.

A grim picture

FOR READING & MEDITATION - EXODUS 7:14-8:19

'Then the LORD said to Moses, "Pharaoh's heart is unyielding;
he refuses to let the people go."' (7:14)

Earlier we mentioned that the book of Exodus frequently
makes connections with the book of Genesis, and the
plagues are a case in point. The plagues are understood by
some as the *reversal of creation*. Consider carefully this
next statement: *God gives people over to the consequences
of their rebellion against the creation order.* He does so in
the Exodus story, as the commentator Peter Enns puts
it, by 'the unleashing of anti-creation forces upon the
helpless Egyptians'.

The first nine plagues are in three groups of three, the
first of each series beginning 'in the morning'.
This literary arrangement helps us to see that the
plagues form a pattern of purposeful, not random,
events. The grim picture is of unrelenting waves
of judgment. The first plague – turning the water
to blood – is notable since the River Nile was
where Pharaoh had drowned the Israelite babies
and because the Nile was Egypt's main artery.
To strike at the Nile was to strike at the heart of
Egyptian life and livelihood. Whatever we do, we
must not fall into misunderstanding the plagues
as normal natural disasters. These events were
unique and purposefully brought about; they
demonstrated for all time God's powerful creative pre-
eminence over the forces of nature.

To believe that God acts on a quid-pro-quo basis is to
have a distorted view of the true picture. Scripture shows
us that God makes the sun to shine and rain to fall on the
righteous and the unrighteous (Matt. 5:45). Sometimes, to
our disappointment and confusion, God does not arbitrarily
'zap' His enemies. And how thankful we should be that He
doesn't – or where would any of us be?

FURTHER STUDY

Rom. 1:18-32;
Acts 26:9-18

1. What happens
when people
reject God?

2. How does
God respond
to those who
reject Him?

**Father, I stand in awe of Your power and Your eternal resources.
How glad I am that I am the recipient of Your grace, not Your
judgment. As long as eternity lasts I shall never cease to praise
You for this. Amen.**

God reigns supreme

FOR READING & MEDITATION – EXODUS 8:20-10:29

'Then the Lord said to Moses, "Go to Pharaoh, for I have hardened his heart ..."' (10:1)

During the ninth plague, 'creation' in Egypt is plunged back into primeval darkness and the Egyptian sun god, Ra, is discredited. As the sun goes down over Egypt so Pharaoh's idolatrous power is eclipsed! But notice, however, that this reversal of creation does not affect the Israelites; we are told they 'had light in the places where they lived' (10:23).

As the darkness of death shadows the land, Pharaoh's heart turns to stone. The account says, 'But the Lord hardened Pharaoh's heart ...' (10:27). Nine times in Exodus Pharaoh is said to have hardened his heart against God, and nine times *God* is said to have hardened Pharaoh's heart. In the first five plagues Pharaoh was responsible for his own hardness towards God, and it is only with the sixth plague that we read God *specifically* hardened his heart (9:12). Does this imply an intensification by God of what was already happening in Pharaoh's heart, confirming him in his own attitudes? That is the generally accepted view, but all along the narrative has anticipated that God would harden Pharaoh's heart (4:21; 7:3). God always intended to make an example of Pharaoh (see 9:16) in the interests not just of Israel but of His larger plan to bring salvation to all nations, including Egypt!

We cannot resolve all the mysteries of Scripture and we need to learn to be comfortable with the tensions it creates. God, it seems, resolves not only to free Israel but to make an example of arrogant, totalitarian power. The good news is that not even the malevolent, self-serving decisions of the most powerful ruler on earth can thwart God's purpose in the end. God reigns supreme. Always.

FURTHER STUDY

Exod. 8:8-15;
Rom. 9:14-25

1. Who hardened Pharaoh's heart?

2. How did Pharaoh's judgment display God's mercy?

O God, once again I bow as I see that You stand as Ruler with supreme authority over all things. Just as Your purposes for Israel could and will not be thwarted, so Your purposes for my life cannot be thwarted. I rest content in that. Amen.

FOR READING & MEDITATION – EXODUS 11:1-12:13
'... when I see the blood, I will pass over you.' (12:13)

The final devastating divine judgment to fall on Egypt is the death of all its firstborn. God, however, promises to preserve the Israelites, assuring them that 'not a dog will bark' at them (11:7). By so doing, God identifies them uniquely as *His* people. In these circumstances one can imagine the Egyptians pleading with the Israelites to leave the land and plying them with gold as an incentive. But the text presents Israel as having gained civic and popular approval (11:3,8) which enabled them to plunder the treasures of Egypt (12:36). It would seem that just as God had hardened the heart of their ruler so He softened the hearts of the general populace.

More specifically, the Israelites are instructed to prepare for their miraculous protection by daubing their doorposts with the blood of the lambs they were to sacrifice so that, when the Lord on His mission of judgment sees the blood, He will 'pass over' their houses. This judgment, which Israel is spared, has caused many to question God's character and goodness. The only mitigation offered in the passage is the very important statement that God's controversy is not with things Egyptian, nor even with Pharaoh himself, but with the *gods* of Egypt (12:12). Pharaoh was a front for false gods, and tragically the people he represented suffered with him and because of him.

From the dawn of time the biggest conflict has been the battle between the true God and all false rivals to His unique glory and place. When will the devil and his emissaries learn that the Almighty will not allow anyone to usurp His authority and position in the universe? God's justice will ultimately prevail, and His peace will ultimately reign.

FURTHER STUDY

John 1:29;
Heb. 9:22;
1 Pet. 1:18-21

1. Why is Jesus called the Lamb of God?

2. What can blood achieve that gold cannot?

Gracious and redeeming God, You who passed over the blood-soaked doorposts of Your people Israel and saved their firstborn, how glad I am that the blood of Your Son has spared me from eternal judgment. Blessed be Your name for ever. Amen.

Empowering worship

FOR READING & MEDITATION - EXODUS 12:14-30

'Then the people bowed down and worshipped.' (v.27)

The feast of Passover, established to commemorate Israel's deliverance, became the central festival of freedom which annually reminded the Israelites that they were the redeemed of the Lord. It was effective because ritual helps to engage memory. *Remembering* connects later participants to the original historic liberation. The Passover ceremony, in effect, makes the exodus redemption more meaningful for present generations of worshippers as they eat unleavened bread and the meat of a lamb which has been sacrificed.

FURTHER STUDY

Deut. 16:1-8;
1 Cor. 11:23-26

1. What is the meaning of Passover?

2. What is the meaning of the Lord's Supper?

In Jewish households Passover begins by one of the youngest children asking, 'What does this ceremony mean to you?' (12:26). The answer then given is in the form of a story – the story of how God passed over the homes in Egypt and led His people from slavery to freedom. For practising Jews this is always a moving and solemn ritual.

The subject of ritual in Christian worship is a controversial one. One view says 'We should dispense with ritual for it endangers our true identity and cuts us off from current means of grace.' What would happen, we wonder, if we began our Holy Communion services by getting a little child to stand up and ask, 'What does this ceremony mean to you?' And what would happen if the pastor or priest then told afresh the story of Jesus, the Passover Lamb, whose death on the cross brought us from bondage to freedom? Some might regard that as ritualistic, but I wonder if it might lead to a more meaningful time of worship. Think how many divisions in the Church might have been avoided if we had answered the question of what goes on in the Supper by telling the story of our Passover Lamb.

Father, forgive us if we regard Holy Communion only as a ritual and do not see beyond it. We ask that You save us not from necessary rituals but from ritualism. May the wonder of what You have done for us continually wash over us. Amen.

Every Day with Jesus
Around the World

Every Day with Jesus continues to speak to many thousands of people around the world.

Not only does the English language edition get shipped in thousands to Australia, New Zealand, Singapore, South Africa, Ghana, Hong Kong and many other places, but locally printed versions are also available in India, Kenya and Nigeria. Concurrent translated editions are available in Sri Lanka in Tamil and Sinhala, and regular Serbian translations are available in print and on radio. Add to these the many translated editions (including French, Mandarin, Arabic, Czech, German, Slovak and Serbian) and the numerous compilation editions in, amongst other languages, English, Malayalam and Persian, and the amazing reach and impact of this publication begins to be seen.

Selected meditations are made available on CD; Braille editions are being painstakingly created, and we have also entered the digital arena with eSubscriptions and eBooks.

This one publication, commenced over 40 years ago on the back of a postcard, continues to change lives on every continent.

Why not consider encouraging someone you know with a copy or a gift subscription?
To do so, visit www.cwr.org.uk/store
call +44 (0)1252 784710 or see the order form
at the back of these notes.

The day of deliverance

FOR READING & MEDITATION - EXODUS 12:29-13:16

'During the night Pharaoh summoned Moses and Aaron and said,
"Up! Leave my people ..."' (12:31)

Midnight, and the final judgment falls on Pharaoh's regime. The long night of grief begins for the bereaved in Egypt, but for the Israelite slaves the day of exodus dawns. A frantic Pharaoh summons Moses and Aaron during the night and orders them to leave, conceding to all their requests and even asking them to bestow a parting blessing on him! The Israelites make their escape, clutching the unleavened bread as God has commanded and weighed down with the treasures the distressed Egyptians have thrust upon them. Pharaoh's defeat is complete. He has been paid in full for his genocidal policy and cruel repression. The Israelites leave, as it were, by the 'front door', heads held high and dressed no longer as slaves. Israel's exaltation is Pharaoh's humiliation.

FURTHER STUDY

Isa. 53:1-12;
Heb. 10:1-18

1. What is substitutionary atonement?

2. Why were animal sacrifices inadequate?

At this point in the text the Passover regulations are repeated as if to remind readers that what they are reading is not a piece of ancient history but powerful contemporary theology which urges them as God's people to remember their roots as liberated slaves. The consecration of the firstborn in Israel is a further means of keeping the exodus at the forefront of the nation's mind. In one sense, Israel's firstborn had been spared by the death of Egypt's firstborn; in another sense, the lambs were the substitute. From this time on every firstborn was to belong exclusively to God, though Numbers 3:11-13 tells us that God chose the Levites in place of the firstborn.

It is fitting to remind ourselves that we who have been redeemed owe everything to our divine substitute – God's firstborn Son. Had He not taken our place then judgment would have fallen upon us rather than on Him.

O gracious Father, what love and compassion You showed us when You determined to offer up Your Son as our substitute. All honour and glory be to Your peerless and precious name. Amen.

FOR READING & MEDITATION - EXODUS 13:17-22

'By day the Lord went ahead of them in a pillar of cloud to guide them ...' (v.21)

Israel discovers (as do all redeemed people) that God's initial act of deliverance is the beginning, not the end, of salvation. To live as a disciple is to embark on a journey of adventure. We need reminding of this lest we think our salvation is something that happened a long time ago. Salvation is a gift and an event; it is also a process and goal to be attained. We are both saved and being saved, and are heading for a salvation to be realised when Christ comes again.

On this journey to the promised land, Israel is to set her sights firmly on God Himself, who guides His people. Notice also the strange way in which He shows His understanding of human weakness and apprehension and leads them not by the shortest route, which might involve them in war, but by a longer route. God seems concerned to keep His people moving at all costs. Rudders cannot steer ships that aren't moving. No doubt God could have led His people straight through any opposition, but He chooses not to. Even God is willing to take into account the real political situation and to make allowances for it. Divine guidance does not rule out sensible planning, forethought, alternative choices, contingencies and wise counsel!

FURTHER STUDY

Psa. 23:1-6;
John 10:1-18

1. Where does God lead us?

2. Why does God condescend to guide us?

To keep His people moving while reassuring them of His continuing presence, God goes ahead of them in a pillar of fire by night and a pillar of cloud by day. The Almighty is the true trailblazer, pioneering the way for His redeemed people and sharing their experiences to the full. Do you feel at the moment as though you have lost your way in life? Then fix your eyes on God, who knows the end from the beginning and delights to lead you in His ways.

Loving heavenly Father, my heart rejoices when I think of how You take into account my foibles and weaknesses. I experienced something of love and compassion before I knew You, but never anything like this. Thank You, my Father. Amen.

Fear not

FOR READING & MEDITATION - EXODUS 14:1-31
'They were terrified and cried out to the LORD.' (v.10)

When Pharaoh learns of the Israelites' departure he has second thoughts and shows himself in his true colours. To lose the Israelite slaves is to lose his cheap source of labour. Without their 'services' the Egyptian economy is threatened. So, in a dramatic U-turn, the Egyptians unleash the army in pursuit. God's strategy now is to lure Pharaoh's army into a trap by what seems on the surface poor military tactics – marching Israel to the sea leaving no route for escape.

The Israelites' reaction shows them in their true colours also. They, too, have a quick change of mind and

FURTHER STUDY

Matt. 14:22-33;
Heb. 12:1-3

1. Why did Peter sink?

2. Where should we look?

claim they would have preferred to have stayed in Egypt; slavery seems a better deal than death in the desert! How quickly we forget. Moses' response is at once a rebuke and a reassurance. In fact, as the people's representative, Moses is in the firing-line for God's own rebuke. The Lord doesn't waste words. His message is, 'Stop complaining. Raise your staff and watch for My glory.' The rest, as they say, is history!

How is it that the Israelites have been so fearful when they had already witnessed many evidences of God's power and greatness? We see in our text for today that 'they were terrified'. It wasn't the enemy without that caused them consternation; it was the enemy within. Of all the things that destroy inner unity fear is, without doubt, the most debilitating. Once we take our eyes off God and allow them to focus on other things then fear soon begins to take over. God's call to His children throughout Scripture is to fear not. Whatever He asks us to do in His name, we need not be afraid, for the Great I Am is with us.

Father, I accept that my greatest enemy is not the enemy without but the enemy within - fear. Take from my inner consciousness all traces of fear. Do it now, dear Father. In Jesus' name. Amen.

A song in two parts

FOR READING & MEDITATION - EXODUS 15:1-21

'Who among the gods is like you, O Lord?' (v.11)

The natural response to redemption is praise, however we should remember that God does not need praise in order for Him to function, as a vain person might need compliments. Just as a beautiful painting or a glorious sunset invokes in us admiration, so our Creator, whose every thought concerning us is good, invokes our praise. Praise and worship are our main reasons for living.

The people of God, having been delivered by God's power, stand on the banks of the Red Sea, awed and relieved by their great escape. Relief soon turns to song as, led by Moses, they celebrate the Warrior who has fought His people's battles for them, and won a stunning victory over their enemies. Miriam, Moses' sister, leads the women with tambourines and dancing in glad response. This song sets a standard for biblical praise and is in two parts. The first part (vv.1-12) focuses on the deliverance from Egypt, and the second part (vv.13-18) focuses on the entrance into the promised land. The Israelites recognised that the total exodus experience consisted not only of coming *out* of Egypt but also involved entry *into* the promised land.

FURTHER STUDY

Eph. 4:17-32;
Col. 1:9-23

1. What are we to put off and put on?

2. What were Paul's two parts of the gospel?

This theme is echoed in the New Testament. Redemption is not only from sin but also *into* the new life that is in Christ. We are not just saved from sin but saved to take possession of the thrilling inheritance that has been made ours by Jesus. Has this truth really gripped your heart? Many Christians see their salvation only in terms of having been forgiven, and have little awareness of what lies ahead. God longs to bring you into the promised land. Have you been brought out of Egypt? Good. Now press forward into Canaan's land.

O Father, help me see my own spiritual exodus in the terms I have read about today - as not only being saved from the past but being brought into new life in Christ. Lead on my Father. I will follow. Amen.

The bitter made sweet

FOR READING & MEDITATION – EXODUS 15:22-27

'He threw [a piece of wood] into the water, and the water
became sweet.' (v.25)

On their journey from slavery to the promised land, we
find the people of God now coming to an abrupt halt.
Singing dies on the desert air, dancing stops, tambourines
are stowed away, the cheering ceases, and we are in the
middle of a survival story – the first of several! Praise
turns to grumbling as they realise that the journey will be
tough. Suddenly the old slavery from which they had cried
to be released begins to look attractive.

It's amazing how quickly our mood of praise can change
and we return to the old pattern of complaint. Once again

**FURTHER
STUDY**

Ruth 1:1-22;
4:13-17

1. How did
tragedy affect
Naomi?

2. How did
God sweeten
her life?

God works a miracle: the wood thrown into the
water causes the rancid pool to become sweet.
Will they – and we – ever learn to trust this God
of grace? There is always, it seems, another test
of faith around the corner. The writer Terence
Fretheim says that adult spirituality is put to the
test in the wilderness 'where evil spirits haunt and
resources run out'. Here at Marah the lesson to
be learned is that of dependent trust. But we also
find a brand-new definition of freedom. To be free
is not simply to be delivered from an oppressive
bondage so that we can do what we choose; it is
to trust the choices that God makes, which are always in
our best interests.

This test of faith is intended to reveal a new facet of
God's gracious provision. And it does. God discloses to His
people a new name: 'I am the LORD, who heals you' (v.26).
What new aspects of God's nature might we discover if
we trusted and travelled with more faith? The journey
which God's people have embarked on is not simply to the
promised land but deeper into the promises of God. How
will God reveal Himself to you today?

**Father, as I read of the wood turning the bitter waters sweet,
how can I not help but think of the cross? That 'old rugged cross'
has touched the bitter waters of my life and turned everything
sweet. My gratitude just won't go into words. Amen.**

Living up to His name

FOR READING & MEDITATION - EXODUS 16:1-36
'The Israelites ate manna for forty years ...' (v.35)

Having complained about the lack of drinking water, the pilgrims now complain about the lack of bread. Once again, in the words of writer, Fretheim, 'a food crisis becomes a faith crisis'. The Israelites fear that they will starve to death in a vast wilderness. Anxiety about how to keep body and soul together is quite natural, but in Israel's case the matter becomes another test of trust.

Can faith stand the strain of freedom? Not easily. Like the Israelites we too may find freedom scary. We cast around for someone to blame or for some false security to cling to. And our deep longing for security often makes us hanker after rules and order even when those rules and principles are sinful ones. How sad that sometimes we prefer our old addictions, our damaging destructive habits, to the challenges of being free. What is more, this deep nostalgia for 'Egypt' causes us to remain immature.

Again God is gracious to His people and promises to provide bread from heaven. Even this is to be a further test of faith to see 'whether they will follow my instructions' (v.4). The bread given is strange. The term 'manna' means 'What is it?', but it saves the day. Notice, *enough* is to be gathered for the day (v.4). The Israelites were to gather just what they needed for the day – no less and no more. There was to be no hoarded grace, no stockpiled faith here (except on the day before the Sabbath). 'Give us *today* our daily bread' is what we are told to ask in faith in the Lord's Prayer (Matt. 6:11). While reflecting on this miracle of provision cast your mind back to what God said about His name to Moses: 'I will be what I will be' (3:14). Did He not live up to His name?

FURTHER STUDY

John 6:5-13, 43-58

1. Compare the Israelites and Andrew.

2. In what sense is Jesus like manna?

Gracious Father, I am so thankful that I worship a God who lives up to His name. Your faithfulness is my security, Your consistency my strength. I breathe more freely now for I know You will never fail me. Thank You, dear Father. Amen.

Water from the rock

FOR READING & MEDITATION - EXODUS 17:1-7

'... the Israelites ... tested the LORD saying, "Is the LORD among us or not?"' (v.7)

As we continue to walk through the wilderness with the newly freed Israelites it is not difficult to imagine the tension they felt and the challenges to faith they encountered. Their feelings were maybe similar to those of a modern motorist who, low on petrol, has just swept past the last refuelling stop before a very long motorway! The challenge which pilgrim people face is to live in the period of time between the promise and the fulfilment.

On this occasion their grumbling at the lack of water is more serious because the testing of their faith leads them to test God. 'Is the LORD among us or not?' they ask (v.7). There is nothing wrong with this question in itself. After all, isn't it a question each of us asks when we long for a sense of the Lord's presence among us? But here the question is not just an innocent longing but a challenge to God to give them proof of His presence. It masks a demand that God prove Himself to be God. This is an attempt to force God's hand so that He demonstrates His power at our insistence and on our terms. This is what the sin of testing God is all about.

Tragically and ironically, the place names which might have commemorated God's miraculous provision instead are a record of Israel's mistrust and presumption! 'Massah', which means 'testing', and 'Meribah', which means 'quarrelling', go down in Israel's sad archives as landmarks of unbelief. As for us, we need to learn the wisdom of walking by the Spirit in that balance of faith between the 'now' of what we already possess of God's kingdom and the 'not-yet' of all that still awaits us in the 'promised land' of His coming kingdom. God asks us to be patient and not to forget that He is with us even as we wait.

FURTHER STUDY

Psa. 95:1-11;
1 Cor. 1:18-25

1. How does the psalmist combine praise and warning?

2. What proof of God are we to preach?

My Father, it is so easy to criticise Your people for their insensitivity and lack of trust in the wilderness, but I must ask myself: How do I react to crises? Am I convinced that You will be all that I need You to be? Help me, Father. Amen.

Uplifted hands

FOR READING & MEDITATION - EXODUS 17:8-16

'As long as Moses held up his hands, the Israelites were winning ...'
(v.11)

The famous incident we reflect on today shows us again that mystery of the intermingling of divine activity and human endeavour which is part of the life of faith. As long as Moses held his staff aloft, Israel, under Joshua's leadership, prevailed over the Amalekites. When he tired and lowered his arms, Israel risked defeat. So Aaron and Hur sat him on a stone and supported his arms.

Israel's steps were dogged by the Amalekites until after the time of King David. The real enemies of the people of God are not those who annoy us with irritating remarks but those who seek to withstand God's redemptive purpose for the world. And when we come up against them conflict is inevitable.

But why did the uplifted arms of Moses represent victory? Most commentators believe they were a symbol of prayer. Yet though no doubt Moses prayed, it is more likely that when he lifted up the staff it acted as a 'rallying point' for Israel, echoing the way in which it had been the sign of God's power in the plagues. The uplifted staff led to victory in the battle. As the Israelites saw it they would have been reminded it was a powerful symbol of God's saving presence and that He was watching and caring for His people. Not for the last time did outstretched arms on a hill determine the outcome of a battle!

FURTHER STUDY

Rom. 15:30-32;
Eph. 6:10-20;
1 Tim. 2:1-8

1. How do we battle in prayer?

2. What did Paul urge?

All of this was to be engraved on Israel's national memory, commemorated on a scroll and in the stone of an altar (vv.14-16). Israel needed to remember that God was not only ready to deliver them from Egypt, provide food and water for them in a wilderness, but to fight for them in their battles too. Are you at this moment facing a battle in which you need divine help? Then be assured, help is on the way.

O God my Father, I come to You for help. The battles I face are more than a match for my puny strength. Save me from my enemies and deliver me not only for my sake but for the glory of Your peerless name. Amen.

The art of delegation

FOR READING & MEDITATION - EXODUS 18:1-27

'Moses listened to his father-in-law and did everything he said.'
(v.24)

We all carry, it has been said, our spiritual history with us. This was certainly true of Moses. It was enshrined in the names he had given his sons. 'Gershom' reminded him of his time in Midianite territory: 'I have become an alien in a foreign land' (v.3); 'Eliezer' of the way God had helped him in the past: 'My father's God was my helper; he saved me from the sword of Pharaoh' (v.4). What spiritual history do you carry with you? Do you think of the good things that have happened to you, or just the seemingly bad things? Remember, no matter how bad something may appear to be, a Christian will find that God can turn it to good.

FURTHER STUDY

Luke 9:1-17;
Acts 6:1-7

1. How did Jesus delegate?

2. How did the Early Church delegate?

In this chapter we also see Moses' wife, Zipporah, rejoining Moses along with Jethro, his Midianite father-in-law. When Jethro is told the good news of Israel's exodus and salvation he becomes a worshipper of Yahweh (vv.9-12). This elderly man proves to be extremely wise. Moses was the pastor of the flock but the queues were lengthening at the counselling tent! Jethro warns Moses he will wear out both himself and the people, and advises delegating the task of listening to their disputes. Moses would then be free to talk to God on their behalf.

Three things become clear from the record. First, if we allocated our responsibilities according to our gifts we might more effectively build up God's people. Second, if we talked more to God than to the people who come to us about their problems we might be of greater help to them (v.19). Third, if we all obeyed more closely the laws God has given us and stopped relying on the wisdom of others we might have less need of counsel (v.20). As our Lord said, 'He who has ears to hear, let him hear' (Matt. 11:15).

Father, help me learn these three lessons - not just in my head but in my heart. Show me what I can and what I cannot do, and help me never become overcommitted so that my health and family suffer. In Jesus' name. Amen.

On eagles' wings

FOR READING & MEDITATION – EXODUS 19:1-4

'You yourselves have seen what I did to Egypt, and how I carried you on eagles' wings ...' (v.4)

Today we finally arrive with Israel at Mount Sinai and begin to consider the momentous events which occurred there – events which transformed Israel into a nation and God's covenant partner. But first, notice how God beautifully pictures the history of His relationship with Israel: 'I carried you,' He says, 'on eagles' wings.' Consider what He had done for them: He had raised up Moses to lead them, delivered them from Egypt, performed wonders and signs to break Pharaoh's resistance, brought them through the Red Sea, provided them with bread and water, and, at last, had guided them to this mountain.

The phrase 'carried on eagles' wings' has within it the music of God's grace. Sometimes Christians contrast the Old Testament God of law with the New Testament God of grace. But that, I believe, is quite wrong. Israel was never intended to work her passage to covenant fellowship with God by doing good works. Rather, as we shall see, the law was given to a people already delivered and brought into a relationship with God. 'Twas grace that brought them safe thus far' and it was by grace that they would be led home. Now grace was set to turn the relationship that already existed into covenant partnership through the giving of the law.

FURTHER STUDY

Deut. 32:7-14

1. What was not with Israel?

2. How does God carry and lead us?

If we compare today's text with Isaiah's word to the fleeing Babylonians, who carried their idols with them (Isa. 45:20), we are then forced to consider the question: do we carry our god, or does our God carry us? Our answer makes all the difference in the world! May I ask you: how many unnecessary religious burdens are you bearing? The true commands of God are not burdensome! They are what wings are to a bird.

Father, help me answer this question truthfully: are You carrying me or am I trying to carry You? Forgive me if I am trying too hard to be a Christian instead of relaxing and resting in Your love. Carry me, dear Father. In Jesus' name. Amen.

'Treasured possession'

FOR READING & MEDITATION - EXODUS 19:1-4
'... I carried you on eagles' wings and brought you to myself.' (v.4)

We linger on this verse to further explore the issue we touched on yesterday, namely that it makes a great difference if the God who commands us is the same God who carries us. But that He *does command us* is a fact we must face squarely.

Obedience, of course, is almost a swear word these days. A wave of anti-authority feeling seems to be sweeping across the world. Contemporary culture has taught us to believe that the self is autonomous, answerable to no one. This attitude has been reinforced by our therapeutic society

FURTHER STUDY

Deut. 10:12-13;
11:13-32

1. Why are God's commands for our own good?

2. What choice does God give us?

whose ideas tend to turn us in on ourselves and make us more self-centred than other-centred. Generally speaking, God-consciousness and neighbour-awareness are things of the past. It may be hard for many in this generation to see that willing obedience to the commands of God is the pathway to fulfilment and human wholeness – but it is. You will probably be familiar with Descartes' famous dictum, 'I think, therefore I am.' This now seems to have been updated to, 'I feel, therefore I am.' The Jewish scholar, Abraham Heschel, speaking from a strong faith viewpoint, said that the right attitude to life should be, 'I am commanded, therefore I am.' To live in obedience to the commands of God is the secret of effective living.

The Israelites who first entered Egypt, went to find bread, but ended up making bricks under the harsh commands of their masters. Those commands were irksome. God's commands, however, bring release – they free us to become the kind of people He intends us to be. We make the paradoxical point once more: freedom is found in servitude. The more we obey God's commands the more free we shall be.

Gracious Father, I am so thankful that not only do You require me to obey Your commands but You provide the power by which I can do so. Help me never to forget this. In Jesus' name. Amen.

'My covenant'

FOR READING & MEDITATION - EXODUS 19:5

'Now if you obey me fully and keep my covenant ...
you will be my treasured possession.' (v.5)

After reviewing the history of their relationship with Him up to the present moment – a history in which Israel has been borne along on the wings of grace – God states His intention to make this bunch of ex-slaves His partner in what He calls *'my* covenant'. By calling it 'my covenant' God not only claims exclusive ownership of the arrangement but reminds Moses that it had existed prior to this meeting at Sinai.

Earlier we saw that God delivered His people because of the promises He had previously made with the patriarchs (2:24; 3:15). Here God is emphasising that He is entering into a covenant relationship with Israel in order to take things a stage further. In the original covenant promise made with Abraham God promised to bless Abraham and through him bless all the nations of the earth. To this end God calls Israel His *treasured possession*. Israel is His personal property, which is what the Hebrew word *segullah* literally means. The idea of value is present too. No doubt you have a 'treasured possession' in your home – a family heirloom or a piece of jewellery perhaps. God has a treasured possession also – His redeemed people (see also Mal. 3:17).

FURTHER STUDY

Deut. 7:6-9;
1 Pet. 2:4-10

1. How does God feel about you?

2. How do you feel about God?

But in case Israel should ever misconstrue this special place in God's heart as being an exclusive, self-centred or nationalistic relationship, the text adds this: 'the whole earth is mine'. God has His sights firmly fixed on *all* the nations, even at the precise moment when He chooses one nation to serve Him in the world! Israel is, undoubtedly, the jewel in God's crown, but the crown God wears is not that of a tribal or even a national god, but the One Creator God of all the world.

O Father, just to be the recipient of Your grace is more than we, Your people, deserve, but to be 'treasured' is almost more than my mind can take in. It is too good to be true. Yet too good not to be true. I am so deeply thankful. Amen.

A priestly kingdom

FOR READING & MEDITATION - EXODUS 19:6
'... you will be for me a kingdom of priests and a holy nation.' (v.6)

Yesterday we unpacked the thought that God chose one nation for the sake of the whole world. This note of special privilege continues when Israel is called 'a kingdom of priests'. What a startling new kind of kingdom this is to be. In it God's people will enjoy living under His direct rule and kingship. But they do so as His priests. In some mysterious way Israel was called to intercede for the world, to echo the groaning of the nations after redemption, and, in an even more mysterious way, to embody the world's sin and suffering on God's behalf. In the end, of course, only one true Israelite, our Lord Jesus Christ Himself, the final priestly king, was able to do this.

FURTHER STUDY

2 Cor. 5:17-21;
Eph. 6:19-20;
Rev. 1:4-6

1. What are the privileges of a Christian ambassador?

2. What are the responsibilities?

God's children have a priestly ministry too. A priest is essentially a mediator between God and people. As a priestly kingdom, Israel is entrusted with God's message so that others might come to know the one Creator God. Notice that Israel is blessed in order to pass on God's blessings to others. What a challenging vocation.

The temptation for God's people in this day and age – as it was for Israel – is to forget our calling to bring blessing to others and turn God into our exclusive possession or make religion into a private, self-serving experience. We are God's ambassadors, chosen for a mission – to represent God to the world and to proclaim the return of King Jesus. But the priestly calling inevitably works the other way too. Not only are we to represent God to the world but we are to represent the world to God, to intercede for it, to feel its sins and carry its sorrows into the eternal presence through prayer. Ours, too, is the function of priesthood.

Father, how can I thank You enough for the privilege of representing You before the world and the world before You? Give me the grace I need to fulfil this awesome responsibility. In Jesus' name I pray. Amen.

The national charter

FOR READING & MEDITATION - EXODUS 19:6

'... you will be for me a kingdom of priests and a holy nation.' (v.6)

We spend another day reflecting on Israel's amazing vocation – to represent God before the world and the world before God. One of the biggest obstacles to our understanding the Old Testament – indeed, the whole Bible – is our modern preoccupation with individual salvation. It is hard sometimes for us to grasp how much God and the biblical writers think in corporate terms. Read carefully this next sentence: *our salvation, while intensely personal, is not individual.* The book of Exodus is not simply the story of how God freed the slaves from Egypt. Rather, the exodus story shows us the lengths to which God is willing to go to create for Himself a people to bring Him glory and through whom He can show to the world something of His awesome character.

FURTHER STUDY

2 Cor. 6:16-7:1;
1 Pet. 2:11-17

1. How can we perfect holiness?

2. How are we God's shop window?

Exodus reminds us most powerfully that God saves individuals with a view to making them into *His holy nation.* God had promised in Genesis 12:2 to make Abraham into a 'great nation', and now Abraham's descendants, the sons of Jacob – at this point a ragged band of former slaves – are being transformed into a nation unlike any other, a nation devoted to God, His glory and His praise. Israel was to be a shop window, if you like, through which other nations could look in and see what happens to those who follow God's commands.

Sadly, they failed, and failed miserably, but to change them into a 'holy nation' was always the divine intention. This is why 'Be holy, as I am holy' became Israel's national charter. It is the Church's charter too. God wants us not simply to be His people but His *holy people.* And without holiness, the writer to the Hebrews reminds us, 'no one will see the Lord' (Heb. 12:14).

O Father, forgive us if we have forgotten that Your goal is not simply to make us Christians but to make us Christlike. As He was holy so we must be holy too. Help us be more holy, dear Father. In Jesus' name we ask it. Amen.

Danger - God at work

FOR READING & MEDITATION - EXODUS 19:7-25

'Whoever touches the mountain shall surely be put to death.' (v.12)

Israel's initial response to God's invitation for them to be a holy nation is an unqualified 'Yes' (v.8), but as was so often to happen in Israel's history, and as happens in our own personal experience, having quickly assented to God's word to them their enthusiasm soon wanes.

The spectacular natural phenomena we read about, which accompany God's arrival at Sinai, are only to be expected since He is the Creator of all things. The thunder and lightning point beyond themselves to God's awesome holiness and majesty. So much in our modern world – and sadly in the Church too – contributes to what one theologian has called 'the trivialisation of God'. We may not have stopped believing in God altogether, but we often cut Him down to our size, reduce Him to our dimensions. However, we domesticate God at great risk. It is dangerous to try to make this transcendent God user-friendly. Though we have been embraced by the Trinity and welcomed into their midst we must be careful that we do not lose a sense of awe and reverence for God. Never mistake intimacy with Him for mateyness, especially when it comes to prayer and worship.

FURTHER STUDY

John 15:12-17;
Acts 5:1-11

1. How did Jesus combine friendship and authority?

2. How did the Early Church view God?

The author Annie Dillard has said this about the Church at worship and prayer, 'Does anyone have any idea what sort of power we so blithely invoke? The churches are like children playing on the floor with their chemistry sets, mixing up a batch of TNT to kill a Sunday morning. It is madness to wear ladies' straw hats and velvet hats to church; we should all be wearing crash helmets.' Like Israel, we would do well to consecrate ourselves (v.10) in order to meet with God. Perhaps every church should have a sign over the doorway that reads, 'Danger – God at Work'.

O Father, help me never to forget that You are not only my Redeemer and Friend, but also my Creator and Sustainer. May I come boldly to Your throne of grace but also with reverential fear and awe. In Jesus' name. Amen.

The Ten Commandments

FOR READING & MEDITATION - EXODUS 20:1
'And God spoke all these words ...' (v.1)

Now we come to the passage in which God gives His Ten Commandments. It is interesting to note that these 'ten words', as some ancient writers referred to them, form the only direct speech from God in this part of the book. The rest of the laws are mediated through Moses. More importantly, as Old Testament scholar Chris Wright points out, what really counted at Sinai was not that there was a spectacular *visible* manifestation of God but that there was a *verbal* revelation of God's mind and will. In his words, 'Sinai was a cosmic audio-visual experience, but it was the *audio* that mattered.' It is often said that a picture is worth a thousand words. But our biblical faith, we should remember, is founded on God's *Word*.

FURTHER STUDY

Psa. 119:1-24; Matt. 17:1-5

1. How can we be blessed and free from sin?

2. What verbal instruction did God give in the Gospels?

Malcolm Muggeridge, the writer and broadcaster who was converted in his later years to Jesus Christ, used to say that one of the things that endeared Christianity to him was the fact that 'In the beginning was the Word ... and the Word was made flesh' (John 1:1,14, AV). Had he seen written, 'In the beginning was the video tape,' he said, it would not have meant anything. He believed that it is through the Word – the expression of God's thoughts – that truth is most clearly conveyed.

Forty years after the giving of the Ten Commandments Moses asked Israel, 'Has any other people heard the voice of God speaking out of fire, as you have, and lived?' (Deut. 4:33). In fact, what made Israel unique and especially privileged was that they were the only nation to whom the living God had spoken in this way. Now, miraculously, He has spoken to the whole world in Jesus. We may not have heard God's voice but in Jesus we have certainly heard His Word.

My Father and my God, how thankful I am that You have spoken to me in Christ, the Word who was made flesh. I do not need to see You to know You are there. Your Word in Jesus is enough. Amen.

Ten(der) commandments

FOR READING & MEDITATION - EXODUS 20:2

'I am the LORD your God, who brought you out of Egypt,
out of the land of slavery.' (v.2)

We linger on this opening statement in order to absorb its significance. The God who gave these Ten Commandments, we must remember, is the God who brought His people out of Egypt. The law does not precede God's grace; it is given to a people already redeemed. So these *ten(der) commandments*, as Ron Mehl calls them, reflect God's redeeming love and promote the liberty of the children of God. At the risk of being repetitive, we consider again that these commands are given to guarantee Israel's freedom and to construct a just, free and equal society – the very opposite of the authoritarian, oppressive, slave-driven society of Egypt.

FURTHER STUDY

Psa. 119:25-56

1. How can we experience hope, comfort and renewal?

2. What should our attitude be towards God's laws?

What a tragic mistake our world has made in rebelling against a good and gracious God. We do not become free by breaking His laws; on the contrary, when we reject them we submit ourselves to bondage by our own uncontrolled lusts or society's fashions or, at worst, the oppression of another Pharaoh! As someone has rightly said, ours is not a permissive society; it is a *transgressive society*! Not that the Ten Commandments are meant merely to produce good citizens in a conventional society. Rather, as Old Testament scholar Terence Fretheim points out, they are the means by which God's ordering of chaos at the cosmic level is made real at the social level so that heaven's will is done on earth.

Far from being relics of an outmoded social system, in reality the Ten Commandments are signposts to the renewal of the human community in Christ. They come from the one Creator God as the 'Maker's instructions' for a better world. Let's commit to living as we were designed to live, for the glory of God.

O Father, it may be unrealistic to expect society to want heaven's will to be done on earth, but because You have revealed Yourself to me that is what I long for. May Your will be done on earth through me this day. In Jesus' name. Amen.

No other gods

FOR READING & MEDITATION – EXODUS 20:3

'You shall have no other gods before me.' (v.3)

In the first of the Ten Commandments God insists on having His people's undivided devotion and tells them firmly that there are no rivals to Him. Why do the Ten Commandments begin in this way? Because, though God is the Saviour of Israel, He can save His people only when they give Him their full trust. Strictly speaking, what is commanded here is not monotheism – 'You must worship only one God.' Rather, the emphasis is that among the competing gods only the Lord is worthy of worship. It is as if God is saying, 'There is only one God, and He has redeemed you, cared for you, lifted you on eagles' wings, brought you into His presence. There is just me and no one else! No other god can do for you what I can do.' The Lord alone is worthy of Israel's undivided loyalty and love.

From this commandment flow all the other commandments. Commentator John Durham puts it well: 'The first four commandments set forth the principles guiding Israel's relationship to God; the last six commandments set forth the principles guiding Israel's relationship with the covenant community, and more broadly with the human family.' From this we see clearly that the free, just and loving society God wants His people to enjoy depends entirely on their maintaining a right relationship with Him. In other words, the Ten Commandments reveal both the will and the character of God. We discover from them not only how to live but also what God is like. Israel is entrusted with the sacred task of representing that Godlikeness to the rest of the world. It has been said before but it bears repeating: our task, too, is to communicate to the world not only what God has said but also what He is like.

FURTHER STUDY

Psa. 119:57-96

1. What did the psalmist promise?

2. What did the psalmist request?

O God, deal with anything in me that would prevent me from showing the world what You are like. Help me be a true reflection of the divine image and reveal not only what You have said but also what You are like. In Jesus' name. Amen.

Free from idols

FOR READING & MEDITATION - EXODUS 20:4-6

'You shall not make for yourself an idol ...' (v.4)

'The human heart,' said the Reformer John Calvin, 'is an idol-making factory.' Knowing this tendency of the human heart, God's warning concerning idols is meant to safeguard not so much His transcendence as His ability to relate to us. Idols are scorned throughout the Old Testament, notably by the prophets, for being inanimate objects, unable to speak or hear or communicate with their devotees. But Yahweh is the living God who speaks. As Peter Enns notes, there is a two-fold thrust in these verses: 'Israel is not to do as other nations do by worshipping the idols of their gods, nor are they to do as the nations do by worshipping their own God that way.'

FURTHER STUDY

Psa. 119:97-112; Isa. 44:9-20

1. How does the Word of God benefit us?

2. Why is idolatry illogical?

The fact that God applies to Himself the term 'jealous' should not be interpreted as meaning that He is spiteful or capricious. On the contrary, it conveys how passionately He cares about His involvement with His people and their ongoing and deeply personal relationship with Him. This is an exclusive relationship. We are here reminded also that God is not someone we 'need' but someone we need to worship. It is a call, as one person has put it, 'to stop attempting to get something out of God and instead to bend our lives towards Him'.

The commandments keep us free from the numerous forms of idolatry that destroy our relationship with God. And they show us that He is worshipped not simply by prayers and songs but also by staying faithful in marriage, honouring family bonds, speaking the truth and loving our neighbour. To do these things is as much worshipping God as singing His praises. William H. Willimon and Stanley Hauerwas expressed this thought, 'The commandments are the way we learn to worship the true God truthfully.'

O God, how thankful I am for this 'jealous' love - a love that is passionately opposed to everything that would entice me away from You. I rest secure in the fact that You love me too much to let me be drawn away from You without a fight. Amen.

FOR READING & MEDITATION – EXODUS 20:7

'You shall not misuse the name of the LORD your God ...' (v.7)

To know someone's name in the ancient world was, in effect, to gain some power over them. Not so with God. This word from God in today's verse guards against the mistreatment of His name. God refuses to be used. The Almighty is not manageable and cannot be controlled by harnessing His name. To know God's name was Israel's greatest privilege. God's action against Egypt in liberating His people was with a view to making His name or fame known in all the earth (9:16). The divine name encapsulates God's own character and reputation, and so when He entrusts His name to His people He is actually putting His reputation on the line.

God's name can and has been misused in many ways – by magic or divination, by profanity or false oaths. But it is just as easy to misuse God's name by empty phrases, glib clichés, or by attaching God's name to some course of action or ideology. Blasphemy is speech about God that makes Him a party to our lies, and it is a sad fact that in these times many seem happy to overlook this. The prophet Ezekiel reveals that the Israelites went into exile because they were blaspheming God's name before the watching nations (Ezek. 20:27). Later the prophet said that God would bring His exiled people back to the land He had promised to give them in order that His name might be honoured (Ezek. 36:23). Jesus, you remember, in the Lord's Prayer, made the hallowing of God's name the number one priority (Matt. 6:9).

The best antidote to the tendency to misuse God's name is to constantly keep before us the fact that His name stands for His character. To dishonour His name is to dishonour His character. It is time for us to take God's name seriously.

FURTHER STUDY

Psa. 119:113-128;
Ezek. 36:16-23

1. Who does God reject?

2. What concerns God?

O God my Father, I see that Your character and Your name are one. Help me not to dishonour Your character in any way, but to remember that You are to be honoured in all things. Amen.

Vital

Bible teacher Phin Hall is passionate about helping people know and understand the Scriptures. In a new series of books called *Vital*, Phin explores spiritual disciplines and how they encourage deeper love for the God we serve. We caught up with Phin to find out more ...

[*Every Day with Jesus*:] What drew you to write the *Vital* series?
[Phin Hall:] The roots of this series go back to my days as a youthworker, when the young people jokingly insisted my answer to everything was, 'Read the Bible and pray'. Behind the joke, however, was a genuine desire to understand why these disciplines were so important and if there were other things they could do to help them as young Christians. So I set about investigating what was so vital about these practices and what else might assist our walk with God.

What was your vision for the series as you began to write?
In life in general, my primary desire is to walk well with God and help others to do so too, so really this has been my vision for this series. The books are for anyone who wants to grow

in their love for God and in their life as one of His children. Each book in the series contains four studies, including daily readings for the individual, followed by questions to ponder or to discuss in groups.

Which disciplines do you cover and how did you select these?

The areas of spiritual discipline I have chosen for this series can be grouped into four areas. Firstly, our focus on God through worship, Bible study, meditation and prayer. Secondly, our focus on others through fellowship, submission, service and witnessing. Thirdly, our focus on ourselves through simplicity, giving, battling temptation and fasting. And finally, our focus on daily life through solitude, silence, thanksgiving, confession and living for today.

These areas of spiritual discipline have been practised for thousands of years by godly men and women, and have been proved of great worth because they bring us into a closer relationship with God.

Scan with your smartphone for extra video material on *Vital*.

Vital: Worship
Worship, Fellowship, Simplicity, Solitude and Silence

Vital: Bible Study
Bible Study, Giving, Submission and Giving Thanks

by Phin Hall
£4.99
Available April 2013

 Also available in eBook/Kindle formats

vital:

Free to rest

FOR READING & MEDITATION - EXODUS 20:8-11
'Remember the Sabbath day by keeping it holy.' (v.8)

The next commandment deals with keeping the Sabbath. It was this commandment that largely defined Israel's life as a holy nation. As we shall see, it almost becomes the badge declaring their covenant identity. The Sabbath was a gift. It offered a day of freedom and space to a people who still remembered the relentless slave-economy of Egypt. It was made to help us preserve our human dignity. To keep the Sabbath blesses us, as we are freed from the unbroken cycle of work and enabled to refresh ourselves and reclaim time for God.

FURTHER STUDY

Psa. 119:129-136;
Matt. 12:1-13

1. What upset the psalmist?

2. What should we do and not do on the Sabbath?

In our modern work-driven, consumerist world, Sabbath-keeping becomes harder and harder. Pressure to succeed and relentless advertising feed our desire to be 'better' and have more, and so this encroaches on every bit of our time and space. But we must realise that rest is a moral issue. Every day we spend in the presence of God and the Lord Jesus Christ is special, of course. But to keep the Sabbath is to honour the rhythm of work and rest that God has built into the order of creation. To stop working, to switch off the PCs, to forego the journey, to stop shopping, is to discover God's rest! It is to enter into the joy of the Lord and to share His sense of satisfaction at creation's completion and goodness.

Most Christians celebrate Sunday as the Sabbath in recognition of the fact that Jesus rose from the dead on the first day of the week. Sabbath celebrated the completion of the old creation; Sunday celebrates the inauguration of the new creation. On this day we are invited to look forward to our share in the ultimate 'rest' of God when we will rest from our labours (Rev. 14:13), and by so doing demonstrate that we are worshippers first and workers second.

Father, I am thankful that I can enter into Your rest. Help me not miss the importance of doing so and forgive me if I have put work before worship. In Jesus' name. Amen.

Honouring parents

FOR READING & MEDITATION - EXODUS 20:12
'Honour your father and your mother ...' (v.12)

This commandment may sound outdated in our contemporary society. During a British TV programme which set out to examine the Ten Commandments a commentator remarked, 'Perhaps it's time we had some new ones, ones that fit more easily into modern-day society'. Were the Ten Commandments for a more primitive age, a less sophisticated people? I don't believe so. They were inscribed in stone to suggest their enduring nature. They are God's prescription for a well ordered life and apply as much to this generation as they did to the generation to whom they were first given.

It is interesting to note that the commandment reads, 'Honour your father *and* your mother'. In the ancient world to honour one's mother as well as one's father was a controversial advance, since society was rigidly patriarchal. But God regarded mothers as well as fathers as being deserving of respect. Another matter worth noting is that there is no time limit to this commandment. It is not restricted to a young child who needs to learn obedience; rather, it indicates that we should have a lifelong attitude of respect. As time goes by children are given the chance to show honour by caring for their aged parents. With increased longevity – at least in the Western world – this command becomes more demanding and offers more scope.

FURTHER STUDY

Psa. 119:137-144;
Matt. 15:1-9;
Eph. 6:1-3

1. How did the psalmist cope with trouble?

2. How may religious people dishonour their parents?

Sadly, nowadays the family is being seen as less and less important, but we ought never to lose sight of the fact that it is truly the school of character. Within the confines of the home we learn to relate to the wider world. If we can learn to honour – even forgive – our parents then forgiving and respecting our neighbour will be a lot easier.

Gracious God, relating to parents can sometimes be difficult, as You know. But I accept that I am commanded to honour them. And if forgiveness is needed then I come to You for this. Please help me, my Father. In Jesus' name. Amen.

Pro life

FOR READING & MEDITATION - EXODUS 20:13
'You shall not murder.' (v.13)

Many Christians are divided concerning the sixth commandment. Some say it forbids the taking of human life in any shape or form. Others believe it excludes such things as capital punishment or taking part in a just war and relates only to unlawful killing, for instance, premeditated murder, abortion and euthanasia. Certainly this commandment reveals the high value God places on human life. The Israelites would also have realised that this commandment ruled out blood feuds among themselves. There were to be no more Cain and Abel tragedies.

FURTHER STUDY

Psa. 119:145-152;
1 John 3:11-20

1. How long are God's laws valid?

2. How might we murder people without killing them?

In the covenant God made with Noah following the Flood, He had already made it clear that the taking of a human life represented an attack on the image of God and was an infringement of His rights (Gen. 9:6). The 'sanctity of life' has become a fashionable phrase in certain quarters, but it is not an abstract idea which can be extended to all life forms in some humanistic or sentimental way. It relates here only to the valuation of human life made by a holy God. The giving and taking of life remain within God's jurisdiction and on His terms alone.

This commandment does not, of course, easily solve all our modern ethical dilemmas, but it surely has some bearing on moral matters to do with human life from its beginnings in the womb to its withering in old age or terminal illness. However sophisticated our debate becomes on abortion and euthanasia, we must never lose sight of this word from God. This sixth commandment is not only to be our starting point but is also to be our constant reference point in all our discussions. Human life is precious to God, and it is to be precious to us too.

O Father, in this complex scientific age when so many questions arise that are difficult to answer, help us as Your people to stay close to Scripture and, if we err, help us to err on the side of caution. In Jesus' name. Amen.

Free to commit

FOR READING & MEDITATION - EXODUS 20:14
'You shall not commit adultery.' (v.14)

This commandment, though regarded simply as a prohibition and restriction, was actually given to protect the institution God intended for the benefit of mankind, namely marriage, and consequently family life. Adultery is an act that involves treachery, betrayal and breakdown in commitment.

The widespread fear of commitment is one reason why adultery no longer figures in most people's minds as a moral offence. Unsure of themselves or the world around them, motivated by mood and feelings, fewer people are willing to make a long-term commitment. 'I can't make vows,' they argue, 'I might change and be unable to keep them.' But such an attitude becomes a self-fulfilling prophecy. It is a sure recipe for infidelity, instability and insecurity. The loss of 'long obedience in the same direction' – to quote the philosopher Nietzsche – destroys the conditions in which true character can emerge. People trust less and as a result, have no depth of experience. Instead they are left to the cruel mercy of their own emotions and circumstances.

With everything in our capitalist world being reduced to a matter of consumer choice, it is hard to persuade people that sexuality is an exception. Some Christians in today's Church have allowed themselves to be influenced by the loud voices of the world and consequently do not regard sexuality as an ethical issue at all! Allow me to disagree: sexuality is not a private matter – as is generally assumed now – but is a public issue that affects the whole community. And those who are single and celibate should ensure they do not fall for the lie that living without sexual fulfilment makes you less of a person.

FURTHER STUDY

2 Sam. 13:1-32; Matt. 5:27-28

1. Why may uncontrollable lust destroy people?

2. How did Jesus expand and explain adultery?

O Father, in an age saturated with sex when so many live together outside of marriage, help us as Your people to live according to Your standards, not the standards of the world. In Jesus' name. Amen.

'Affluenza'

FOR READING & MEDITATION - EXODUS 20:15
'You shall not steal.' (v.15)

The eighth commandment protects property by setting limits to our acquisitiveness. Since property is an extension of the self, theft is an assault on another person's privacy and dignity – as any victim of burglary will tell you. This command was especially intended to protect the poorer members of society from the asset-stripping of stronger, more avaricious people. So seriously is this taken that later case-laws provide for legal redress, recompense and restitution. In wider terms, theft can be seen as failure to trust God or, in some cases, a refusal to embrace His calling to useful work.

FURTHER STUDY

Psa. 119:153-160;
1 Tim. 6:6-19;
James 5:1-6

1. Why may rich people have many griefs?

2. Is delaying payment a form of theft?

For those living in the Western world possessiveness presents a challenge. It raises these questions: At whose expense has this wealth been gained? Are workers being underpaid? Are poor workers in the Developing World being exploited to advance Western standards of living? What of those who rig the market, speculate with the currency, or specialise in the financial chicanery that falls only just short of outright theft? In a world sick with 'affluenza' we who name the name of Christ ought to ensure that we have not fallen victims to this disease.

Take a moment right now to examine your own heart to see if there is an acquisitive streak in you that militates against a deep and abiding trust in God. Ask yourself: is it money that controls me or the Master? If you find you are guilty of being driven by the desire for wealth, repent of it and from now on put your whole weight on God. No wonder daily bread, forgiving debts and the threat of temptation figure so largely in the Lord's Prayer. They are issues that take us to the heart of our faith – basic trust.

O God my Father, if this dreadful disease of 'affluenza' has taken hold of me then please help me, I pray. I say 'taken hold of me', but perhaps it would be more true to say that 'I have taken hold of it'. Deliver me and set me free. Amen.

'Truth decay'

FOR READING & MEDITATION – EXODUS 20:16

'You shall not give false testimony against your neighbour.' (v.16)

The world, generally speaking, suffers not only from 'affluenza' but also from *truth decay*. When first given, this commandment applied particularly to the law courts. Justice is at stake when truth is called into question. This word from God seeks to maintain the honesty of judges, the honesty of witnesses, and the validity of evidence. It was later extended to cover personal relationships and so was applied to slander and then, more generally still, to all lies, falsehood and dishonesty. Truthful words build up the community; lying words bring chaos, deceit and distrust.

Think how easily words become devalued. Soap operas so often depend for their dramatic tension on lies, intrigue, concealment and deceit. We mistrust politicians because we are not certain that the spin-doctors are telling us the truth. Propaganda and advertising fuel our sense of unease at whether we can be sure of any claim or promise. The public relations experts say, 'Peace, peace, when there is no peace'!

Failure to speak the truth is again a failure to trust in God. In Christ we need to relearn the lost skill of speaking the truth in love, of walking and talking the truth, of being witnesses to the truth. A day came, as we know, when the Faithful Witness, Jesus, clinched His case by dying for the truth. And over the centuries some of His followers have had to lay down their lives in the interests of truth. How strong is our commitment to truth? For the good of others and for the glory of God, are we willing to stand up against injustice, protect the rights of the disadvantaged and hold to biblical principles which bring life? Can we be part of the antidote to 'truth decay'?

FURTHER STUDY

Psa. 119:161-168;
Eph. 4:29-5:20

1. What benefit do we gain from God's law?

2. What things should we speak and not speak?

O God, give me the courage and power to do the right thing no matter what the circumstances. Help me be so committed to the truth that I will not depart from it either in word or in deed. In Jesus' name I pray. Amen.

Exposing the roots

FOR READING & MEDITATION - EXODUS 20:17

'You shall not covet your neighbour's house ... or anything that belongs to your neighbour.' (v.17)

This last commandment is truly the 'sting in the tail'. If we think the commandments are merely external laws which we need only come close to obeying then this tenth word demolishes any such idea. The Danish philosopher Søren Kierkegaard once astutely observed that we like to think of the Ten Commandments as *intentionally a little too severe* – like putting the clock on half an hour so as not to be late! But this tenth commandment will not allow us to play mental tricks with God's will for our lives. It probes the attitudes of our heart and exposes our underlying motives. It moves the focus from the practicalities of public and domestic life – work, sex, family – to the dark caverns of the human heart. With this last word the commandments are internalised.

When Jesus referred to these laws and added 'But I tell you ...' (Matt. 5:28) He was not overturning these commands but drawing out their inner meaning by exposing what lies at the root of all disobedience, namely covetousness. So to break this commandment was seen as a step which would lead to the violation of all the rest. Israel tragically demonstrated the ingrained tendency to covet what other gods had to offer – and suffered the consequences for it. Similarly, we suffer when we allow desires to grow within us to want other people's property, reputation, spouse, and even their very life. Covetousness breeds discontent and social unrest.

Some regard the Ten Commandments as wholly negative, but in the larger scheme of things they are a firm 'No' to the life lived without God, just as Jesus is the resounding 'Yes' to the promise of life empowered by God and lived for His glory. Again we say, 'He who has ears, let him hear'.

FURTHER STUDY

Psa. 119:169-176; James 3:13-4:7

1. How can God's laws sustain and protect us from harm?

2. What is the result of uncontrolled desire?

O God, if it is necessary, put me through Your detoxification programme which will set me free from all things which cannot satisfy. You are the fountain of life. Help me to draw my health from You. In Jesus' name. Amen.

The fear of the Lord

FOR READING & MEDITATION - EXODUS 20:18-21

'Moses said to the people, "Do not be afraid."' (v.20)

In this passage we see that God has indeed spoken out of the fire, His words minted in the furnace of His holy love for His people. The natural phenomena which gave evidence of His presence among them cause the people to tremble. The smoke coming from the fiery mountain replicates for the people Moses' experience at the burning bush. Getting close to God will never leave us unchanged, because we can be sure that the closer we get to Him the more our fallen state will be revealed in the light of His holiness. So, on one level, it is not surprising that the people preferred to keep their distance. They found even God's voice intimidating and begged Moses to speak to them indirectly as God's spokesman.

'Do not be afraid,' is his first reassuring word. This comforting word, as you are no doubt aware, appears in many places in the Bible. Moses goes on to announce, 'God has come to test you' – not in the sense of finding them out, but in providing them with an experience which will be etched deeply on their memory. Then he adds, '... the fear of God will be with you to keep you from sinning.' What a paradox: 'Don't be afraid' and 'Fear God'!

Carry this thought into the future and it will serve to keep you from sin: *the fear of the Lord produces a strong moral antiseptic in the heart.* We may think we have better, more noble reasons for pleasing God, but when all else fails the fear of the Lord is the most effective. The old hymnwriters Tate and Brady captured the paradox well when they wrote, 'Fear Him ye saints and you will then have nothing else to fear'! The fear of the Lord, it is important to remember, is not a crippling fear which paralyses but a healthy fear that motivates.

FURTHER STUDY

Prov. 2:1-3:12;
9:10-12

1. Define what fear of the Lord is and what it is not.

2. What are the blessings of fearing God?

O Father, I accept that when I fear You I need fear nothing else. Saturate my soul with a godly fear so that no other fear will be able to take root in me. In Jesus' name I pray. Amen.

Rights and responsibilities

FOR READING & MEDITATION - EXODUS 20:22-23:13

'You are to be my holy people.' (22:31)

This large section which covers many aspects of life and illustrates what God wants for His people comprises what is known as the Book of the Covenant. Though we may regard ourselves as remote from some of the situations addressed here, as we read one thing becomes clear: *God is intimately interested in every aspect of His people's daily living.* Holiness is to permeate the very fabric of a people whose destiny it is to be a holy nation.

Once more, we notice the importance of worship, which is both the number one priority and the concluding note of this section. All of life is rooted in worship. It is the prime reason for us being on earth. We call things 'secular' because we have neatly detached God from most spheres of life and confined Him to spiritual game-reserves called 'sacred areas' where we visit Him from time to time. But here the treatment of servants, personal injuries, property rights, and so on, are dealt with – everything is in the end a theological issue, reflecting something of what God is like and how He wants His people to live.

FURTHER STUDY

Col. 3:12-4:1

1. How do Paul's instructions mirror God's commandments?

2. How can we serve God at work, home and church?

Many think (as we have been saying) that when God lays down principles by which men and women should live He is wanting to curtail our freedom. But all God's laws and principles are evidence of His preventive grace. They are like boundaries and fences put up at the edge of precipices to keep us from going over. They do not exist to bind our freedom; they exist to save us from using our freedom to destroy ourselves. God has designed a moral universe, and we cannot evade it or twist it to our own ends. We choose, but because there is a moral order, our choices will always have consequences.

Father, help me accept that I am not God – You are. And Your will, not my will, must be done. Help me to start with You and stay with You – in all things. In Jesus' name. Amen.

The Heart of Worship

To worship is to ascribe 'worth' to what we value most - and no one is more worthy of adoration and praise than God Himself!

Join us in the next issue as we journey through the Bible to the heart of worship. Consider afresh the stories of Job, Abraham and the disciples, which highlight for us some of the barriers to worship and what true worship looks like. Together we will discover:

- Worship as a vital part of our relationship with God
- How to worship whatever our circumstances
- The impact of worship on God, ourselves and our world.

Also available as eBook/ eSubscription

No presumption

FOR READING & MEDITATION - EXODUS 23:14-33

'See, I am sending an angel ahead of you to guard you ...
and to bring you to the place I have prepared.' (v.20)

We continue to look at the laws in the Book of the Covenant. As we noticed yesterday, the social responsibilities urged on Israel are rooted firmly in the worship of the one true God. True worship and viable social life are inextricably interwoven. Neglect one and the other suffers. Worship cleanses us from social failures and regathers us as God's covenant people who are committed to being holy. Righteous and neighbourly behaviour, on the other hand, keeps our worship from being hypocritical and shows how much we love this wonderfully gracious and holy God.

FURTHER STUDY

Luke 13:1-5;
18:9-14

1. What did Jesus explain?

2. What did the Pharisee presume?

God promises the Israelites that He will lead them to the promised land, the place He has prepared for them. Their stewardship of the land, demonstrated in the offerings they are to bring to Him at festival times, will clearly separate them from the idolatrous pagan people around them. This probably explains the otherwise inexplicable cooking instruction in verse 19: 'Do not cook a young goat in its mother's milk' – presumably a Canaanite practice. Equally mysterious is the figure of the angel who has appeared before in Exodus (see 14:19) and is now given the role of going ahead of the people into Canaan, thus representing the presence of God. The warning that there will be no forgiveness for rebellion against Him is thankfully overstated – but God's people needed to hear it. Does this warning make God inconsistent? In other parts of Scripture the Almighty is seen promising forgiveness to the truly repentant. How then can this be explained? I wonder if He wanted the people to understand that He reserves the freedom to forgive when He chooses, but no one dare presume upon it.

O Father, have I reached the point where I take Your forgiveness for granted? If so then burn this truth into my spirit: it is not my merit that has made me who and what I am, but Your mercy. Blessed be Your name for ever. Amen.

The bond-in-blood

FOR READING & MEDITATION - EXODUS 24:1-18

'This is the blood of the covenant that the LORD has made with you in accordance with all these words.' (v.8)

Now we come to the next key stage in the unfolding drama of Israel. At this point God proceeds to ratify the covenant He has made with Israel. One scholar has summarised the sequence of the story from chapters 15 to 24 as care, covenant, commandment and communion. The Israelites needed to learn that communion with a holy God is not only an important matter, but also an awesome and life-changing one. The people as a whole are instructed to stay well back, a smaller group including Aaron, his two sons, and the 70 elders, are invited to move a stage closer, but only Moses is permitted to ascend to the holiest place of all. These three levels of intimacy here at the mountain will be reflected later in the three-section set-up of the tabernacle and the Temple.

Two features particularly merit our attention in this ritual of covenant ratification: *the book and the blood.* Moses reads from the Book of the Covenant and gains the people's assent to what is said in God's Word. Then he sprinkles blood from sacrifices over the people and on the altar, thus confirming the bond-in-blood between God and His people. After that Moses and the group with him 'see' God – and eat and drink in His presence (v.11).

The next time you take Holy Communion and gaze, as the hymnist put it, 'on things unseen', let your mind go back to the section of Scripture we are looking at today and visualise yourself as eating and drinking before God's face. Then, as you partake of the sacred emblems, do it with joy and thanksgiving in remembrance of the fact that what you are doing is reaffirming the bond-in-blood through Jesus, without which none of us would ever dare to approach God's sacred presence.

FURTHER STUDY

Luke 22:14-20; Heb. 9:11-28

1. What did Jesus explain?

2. What does Hebrews explain?

Gracious God, how can I ever thank You enough for this bond-in-blood, this precious pact by which I, a sinner, can come into Your presence forgiven, cleansed, and made whole? Glory be to Your name. Amen.

'The Immanuel principle'

FOR READING & MEDITATION - EXODUS 25:1-27:21

'... have them make a sanctuary for me, and I will dwell among them.' (25:8)

Today we ask ourselves: why was it necessary for Moses to stay 40 days and nights on the top of Mount Sinai? The passage before us now, and the chapters that follow, provide us with the answer. On the mountain, Moses received from God detailed instructions for what has been described as 'The Church in the Wilderness' – the tabernacle – which would be Israel's portable place of worship. Before the tabernacle is constructed, however, God invites His people to have a hand in the matter by willingly giving an offering.

FURTHER STUDY

1 Cor. 3:16-17; 6:19-20; Eph. 2:11-22

1. What did Paul explain?

2. How does God dwell with us now?

The tabernacle is to be a sanctuary for God so that He can *dwell among His people*. How eager He seems to be to accompany His people on their wilderness wanderings. One scholar has called this 'the Immanuel principle at the heart of the covenant'. One day, as we know, 'the Immanuel principle' became a Person in the form of Jesus. How much more with His people can God be than to become one of them?

Notice also that Moses was to build the tabernacle 'according to the plan shown [him] on the mountain' (26:30). This implies that the earthly structure is a symbol of a heavenly reality. Because God is King over Israel, the tabernacle, and later the Temple, not only serve as His earthly address but also as His royal palace! The ark of the covenant – the chief article of furniture in the sanctuary – is later described as the footstool of His throne (1 Chron. 28:2); that is, the earthly footstool of God's heavenly throne. This is an illustration of what happens when we worship – the King of heaven comes among us. How awesome. This realisation has the potential to change our attitude to worship for ever.

Gracious and loving heavenly Father, I am so thankful that Your desire to enter into a relationship with Your human creation led You to come among us. You truly are Immanuel - God with us. Thank You, Father. Amen.

What a Saviour!

FOR READING & MEDITATION - EXODUS 28:1-30:38

'Whenever Aaron enters the Holy Place, he will bear the names of the sons of Israel over his heart ...' (28:29)

You may wonder why we are not adopting the popular approach to the tabernacle which allegorises every detail in an effort to search for spiritual analogies to the Christian life. Our approach this issue is not to deal so much with the question, 'What does the tabernacle suggest about the Christian life?' (something, of course, that is touched upon), but with what it tells us about God and His relationship with His people. Today we consider the issue of the priesthood.

The priest was an important figure in Israel's life and worship; he was the crucial go-between in Israel's relationship with God. The high priest, in particular, was an immensely significant person. Responsibility and representation defined his role. Bearing the names of the 12 tribes on his shoulders, he symbolically took responsibility for them before God (28:9-12). By wearing the names of the tribes on the breastplate over his heart, he symbolically represented them as he went into the Holy Place. Behind the richly ornamented garb and strictly controlled movements of the high priest was the divine intention to facilitate access to the presence of God. Sacrifices were offered, intercessions made, and the priesthood was carefully set apart so that God's rebellious people might come before Him to hear His voice and receive forgiveness in a place consecrated by His glory (29:42-46).

FURTHER STUDY

Heb. 2:10-3:6; 4:14-5:10

1. How did Jesus fulfil the role of high priest?

2. Why did God's Son endure human frailty?

How thankful we should be that Jesus, our great High Priest, has proved able to take the government upon His cross-bearing shoulders, and loving enough to bear the names of repentant sinners over His heart into the Father's presence. What a Saviour!

Father, my heart is full of gratitude for the provision made by Jesus, my great High Priest, who carries my name on His heart as He stands in Your presence. Amen.

Spiritual gifting

FOR READING & MEDITATION – EXODUS 31:1-11

'... I have filled him with the Spirit of God, with skill, ability and knowledge in all kinds of crafts ...' (v.3)

In this remarkable passage we observe God inspiring in His people the skills that were needed to construct the tabernacle. These two otherwise unknown men, Bezalel and Oholiab, become famous by participating in God's work and, more particularly, by the way they were filled with God's Spirit to do so. Not only prophets and charismatic leaders are God's agents in renewal but designers, goldsmiths, silversmiths, embroiderers and woodcarvers also.

Too often we mistakenly associate the Spirit of God only with sensational miracles. But this is to narrow down the scope of His activity and interests. The Spirit is equally the ultimate source of all artistic creativity and craftsmanship which is dedicated to the worship of God. As Philip Yancey points out, the Holy Spirit has a magnificent obsession with the ordinary. Under His influence, what we consider to be merely natural talents and gifts are enhanced and released by His creative energy.

FURTHER STUDY

Acts 9:36-42;
1 Cor. 12:1-31

1. How did Dorcas use her talents for God's glory?

2. What gifts and ministries does Paul identify?

A mother who did not have a promising start in life was sickly as a child and left school early without much of an education. However, by God's grace she became an avid reader who gained a great knowledge of the Scriptures. This knowledge she was able to share with others since she became a valued speaker at women's groups. By the Spirit's enrichment of what we have and do, the order and beauty of God's creation are expressed and God's own glory shines through. Never write yourself off or underestimate what the Holy Spirit can achieve with your meagre stock of natural resources when they are all consecrated to Him.*

Gracious Father, all the powers and gifts I possess by nature are enhanced when touched by Your Spirit. May I no longer see them simply as they are, but as they can be. Heighten them, I pray, so that I shall be at my best for You. Amen.

*For help on this issue, download the free questionnaire *Discovering Your Basic Gift* from www.cwr.org.uk/free-downloads or see *Discovering Your Spiritual Gifts* by Ron Kallmier, available from CWR.

First things first

FOR READING & MEDITATION - EXODUS 31:12-18

'You must observe my Sabbaths. This will be a sign between me and
you for the generations to come ...' (v.13)

It is sometimes said that the opening chapters of the book
of Genesis teach us that human beings are the *crown* of
God's creation. This, of course, is true, but it is equally true
to say that the Sabbath is the *goal* of creation. God's human
creation is indeed the pinnacle of His work, and has been
given exalted responsibility over everything else He has
made. But the Sabbath represents that towards which all
creation – including human beings – is directed.

For Israel, God's immediate Sabbath rest was the
promised land, but this in turn becomes in Scripture a
symbol of the ultimate rest of God's salvation
in the coming kingdom when He 'rests' from His
new creation labours (see Hebrews 4 for a more
detailed explanation of this truth). Israel was to
keep this hope alive in the world by observing
the Sabbath. As God's covenant partner on earth,
Israel kept the Sabbath as a badge of her identity,
stewards of the world's future.

The practical benefits of the Sabbath were
obvious too, with animals and fields included in
the regular respite from work. For the Israelites,
as ex-slaves, the Sabbath was a treasured gift,
reminding them of the grace that had saved
them from the unremitting, round-the-clock
production lines of Egypt's slave economy! Above
all, it was not meant to deprive them – or us – of
fun, or encourage them to be work-shy, but to enable them
to know God better (v.13). Just as God's six-day working-
week dignifies the work we do, so God's Sabbath rest
reminds us weekly that we are called to be worshippers,
not workaholics.

FURTHER STUDY

Luke 14:16-24;
Rev. 2:1-4

1. How can
acquisition,
ambition and
acquaintances
distract us?

2. How can the
work of the
Lord obscure
the Lord of
the work?

**O God, once again I must pause and ask myself: Am I more of
a worker than a worshipper? Does work interest me more than
worship? If so, forgive me and help me put first things first. In
Jesus' name. Amen.**

Israel's fall from grace

FOR READING & MEDITATION - EXODUS 32:1-6, 15-29

'When Joshua heard the noise of the people shouting, he said to Moses, "There is the sound of war in the camp."' (v.17)

Today's reading comes as quite a shock after learning of Israel's redemption and covenant with God. Suddenly an event occurs which threatens to unravel all God's plans. It is tragic to see how quickly Israel turns away from God and falls from grace as she lapses into idolatry. It is not so much that Israel wants another god but that the people want a visible symbol of God's presence. Perhaps they have grown uneasy as a result of Moses' absence. Whatever the reason, they now seek to honour God in an illegitimate way.

FURTHER STUDY

Ezek. 8:1-9:11

1. What was the elders' wrong thinking?

2. Is God's compassion limitless?

Coming down the mountain, Joshua suggests to Moses that there is an unusual sound of war in the camp. But the situation is far worse – it is both more sad and more pathetic. Moses' reply is paraphrased by John Durham in this way: it is 'not the sound of heroes exulting, nor the sound of losers lamenting, but the sound of random singing that I hear'. 'Random singing' is a phrase that could also be used in connection with some contemporary Christians who celebrate but have no victory in their daily lives, who rejoice but have no clear idea of what they are rejoicing over, and know nothing of the other side of drawing close to God, which is lament. In some parts of the contemporary Church it seems that the round of boisterous songs is designed to help people feel good about themselves rather than provide a setting for the worship which God seeks – worship that is 'in spirit and in truth' (John 4:24). Aaron's excuse was that he was going with the flow of popular demand and giving the people what they wanted. But as history vividly illustrates, when idolatry starts you can be sure that immorality isn't far behind!

O God, how weary You must be of our self-interest which is evident even in the way we attempt to praise and worship You. So often we use spiritual songs to lift ourselves up rather than glorify You. Forgive us and restore us. Amen.

Moses' intercession

FOR READING & MEDITATION - EXODUS 32:7-14,30-35

'"I have seen these people," the Lᴏʀᴅ said to Moses, "and they are a stiff-necked people."' (v.9)

Israel's tragic fall from grace, as we saw yesterday, threatens to bring the exodus story to an abrupt end. God has in mind to disown Israel because, as He tells Moses, 'your people, whom you brought up out of Egypt, have become corrupt' (v.7). He has seen not only the people's outward idolatry but also the stubbornness of their hearts. God decides to leave them to face the consequences of their actions and appears to forestall any possible intervention from Moses. '*Leave me alone* so that my anger may burn against them,' He declares. God even seems to be offering to start all over again, with Moses as His new Abraham, because He continues, 'Then I will make you into a great nation'.

Despite Israel's disloyalty, Moses decides to mediate between the people and their God. He pleads mitigation for the people in a moving and justly famous moment of intercession. First Moses reminds God of His saving power in the past. Then he argues that God's reputation is at stake. What will the neighbour-nations think? Above all, he reminds God of His promises made to the patriarchs which are always the reliable bottom-line guarantee of His commitment. As a result the Lord relents.

What a wonderful model prayer this is. Boldly Moses holds God to His own integrity of word and action, and goes as far as to offer his own life in Israel's stead. Prayer calls on God to be God, and as we pray we show our trust in His wonderful character. How amazing, too, that He is willing to be entreated by us and that our prayers change the course of history. Even more amazing, though, is that this same God would one day be prepared to offer His own Son to make atonement for our sins.

FURTHER STUDY

Job 9:33;
Ezek. 22:23-31;
Heb. 7:22-28

1. What does God look for?

2. What is Christ's continuing role?

O God my Father, how encouraging it is to know that powerful intercessory prayer can bring about great changes in history. How encouraging, too, that the channel of prayer is always open. Help me to make good use of it. In Jesus' name. Amen.

Glory!

FOR READING & MEDITATION - EXODUS 33:1-23

'When my glory passes by, I will put you in a cleft in the rock ...'
(v.22)

Yesterday we saw that following Israel's fall God might have altered the plot in the story of redemption were it not for Moses' timely intervention. But the situation is still serious. God refuses to travel any further with His rebellious people in case He destroys them en route! Despite Moses' intercession, then, it seems nothing has really changed. Constructing the tabernacle is a pointless exercise since God will not occupy it. And the first 31 chapters of Exodus are all undone by God's refusal. This could well be the end of the road. Everything hangs in the balance.

FURTHER STUDY

2 Cor. 3:7-4:7;
Heb. 1:1-3

1. How does Jesus reveal God's glory?

2. How do we reveal God's glory?

Again Moses steps into the breach. He hastens to the temporary tabernacle he used for 'face-to-face' meetings with God and pursues God as a faithful friend. In essence he says, 'You want me to lead, Lord, but who will follow me? I may have found favour with You but what about the people, do they have a future?' 'My Presence will go with you,' the Lord replies (v.14). But Moses persists in presenting the people's case. He argues that without God's ongoing presence they would have an unenviable future (v.15). Unless He went with them how would they know they had His favour (v.16)? These arguments are powerful and persuasive, encouraged by God's grace and matched by His response.

Emboldened further, Moses asks to see God's glory, but is allowed only a glimpse of God's back, not His face! This was the closest Moses got to the glory in his lifetime, but a thousand years or more later he stood on another mountain and talked with Jesus, seeing Him transfigured before his very eyes (Matt. 17:3)! What a moment that must have been. However, it is as nothing compared to the glory that will one day be revealed to us all.

O God, help me understand that sometimes when You appear to block me You are doing so not to disappoint me but to develop me - to encourage me to pray more powerfully, with more determination. Teach me more about prayer, Father. Amen.

God's autobiography

FOR READING & MEDITATION - EXODUS 34:1-35

'... the Lord, the compassionate and gracious God, slow to anger,
abounding in love and faithfulness ...' (v.6)

Towards the end of the period in which Moses communed with God on the Mount, the Almighty wrote out for him a second copy of the Ten Commandments. But before so doing He proclaims His name to Moses (v.5). Here God reveals something about Himself that He has not revealed before. This is as close as Israel would come to God's autobiography. The Lord is *compassionate and gracious*, tender towards the suffering and full of unmerited favour, undeserved goodness and unconditional love. How good it is also to know God is *slow to anger*. In the words of the writer Peter Lewes, 'If God were quick to anger we would have been history before we were news!'

God, too, is *abounding in love and faithfulness*. God is full of *hesed* – the Hebrew word for that tough covenant love which perfectly complements His tenderness and guarantees the continuance of the covenant relationship. The outflow of this is God's *faithfulness* – a consistency of purpose and commitment to His promises that reflects His own integrity and His willingness to forgive. However, the second half of verse 7 reminds us that God is not indifferent to sin, that sin results in consequences, and that seeds sown in one generation are often tragically reaped in another.

Moses, seeking reassurance from God about Israel's future, confesses the people's stubborn sinfulness and receives from the Lord a wonderful renewal of the covenant (vv.10–28). Later we read that Moses is seen with his face aglow (v.30). Time spent with God always produces results. The evidence may not always be apparent in our physical features but it will be there in our inner being. Time spent with God is never wasted. So talk on.

FURTHER STUDY

Psa. 86:1-7

1. Define grace, kindness, love, faithfulness, slowness to anger.

2. What do these definitions reveal about God?

O God, I would emerge from my prayer times, perhaps not with a shining face, but with a shining soul, more alive to You, and more alive to others. I would have more of You come in so that more of You can be visible in me. In Jesus' name. Amen.

Shalom!

FOR READING & MEDITATION – EXODUS 35:1-39:43

'Moses inspected the work and saw that they had done it just as the
Lord had commanded.' (39:43)

As we have already noted, our preference in this issue of
Every Day with Jesus is not to try to press the details
given of the tabernacle into some speculative scheme of
interpretation but to stand back and see the big picture. In
fact, the tabernacle is less a coded model of salvation and
more a wonderful *microcosm of creation*. It represents a
creation-in-miniature marked by all the features found in
the first chapter of Genesis.

In particular notice the following: the seven times God
spoke to Moses, ending with the Sabbath; the bringing of
all the rich resources of God's world into order and
beauty; the action of the creative Spirit of God;
the fact that the work is said to be completed; the
way Moses inspects the work, pronounces himself
satisfied and blesses it; the commencement date
on the first day of the first month. All of these
features echo the account in Genesis I. In other
words, just as the Sabbath sanctifies time so the
tabernacle sanctifies space. In the midst of a
fallen, disordered, rebellious world the tabernacle
is one place where the original beauty and design
and purpose of creation as a vehicle for God's
glorious presence can be seen! On this small scale
it is 'just as it was at the beginning'.

**FURTHER
STUDY**

Heb. 9:1-11;
Rev. 21:1-4

1. What did
the Holy
Spirit show?

2. What are the
characteristics
of the new
order?

As a herald of what will yet be, the tabernacle is also a
prophetic parable of what will be at the end in the final
splendour of God's new creation where all will be *shalom*
(perfect peace) and He will dwell with His people for ever.
That day is yet to come, but be assured it will come. What
God begins He always finishes. He's promised He will do
so. And, as the great preacher, C.H. Spurgeon, said, 'The
future is as bright as the promises of God.'

**Father, over the weeks I have come to realise You are sensitising
my inner being, quietly bringing me under the sway of Your
purposes. And nothing thrills me as much as to know the end of
those purposes – *shalom*. I am so grateful. Amen.**

The high point of maturity

FOR READING & MEDITATION - EXODUS 40:1-33

'Moses did everything just as the LORD commanded him.' (v.16)

One statement occurs several times in this section. Did you notice it? It is this: *as the LORD commanded him.* Throughout the construction of the tabernacle Moses was motivated and driven by one all-consuming passion – to do everything just as God had commanded him. There were no shortcuts, no lowering of standards, no cutting of corners. Everything was constructed and crafted *exactly* as God had shown him. What a painstaking and obedient servant Moses proved to be.

Earlier we said that one of the greatest virtues we can possess in relation to God is obedience. It is, as one preacher, put it, 'the high point of spiritual maturity'. What place does obedience have in your life? Are you willing to do what God asks you to do whether you feel like it or not? The apostle Peter tells us that we 'have been chosen according to the foreknowledge of God the Father, through the sanctifying work of the Spirit, for obedience to Jesus Christ and sprinkling by his blood' (I Pet. I:2). Notice that: chosen for obedience. The final achievement in the outworking of God's purpose in redemption is that our lives should be brought into correspondence with His will.

FURTHER STUDY

Gen. 22:1-14;
Rom. 1:5;
Phil. 2:5-8

1. How are faith and obedience linked?

2. What should be our attitude?

When Queen Elizabeth II (the present queen of England) came to the throne she received a wonderful letter from her grandmother, Queen Mary. It was a letter of congratulation from a stately regal figure to a mere slip of a girl. And how did she sign it? 'Your loving grandmother'? No. She signed the letter 'Your devoted and obedient subject'. Is that your attitude too? You may be devoted to God but are you obedient? That is when we really begin to grow as disciples.

Father, help me never forget that the purpose of my redemption is to walk Your way and do Your will. I am truly Your devoted and obedient subject. Amen.

He remains

FOR READING & MEDITATION - EXODUS 40:34-38

'So the cloud of the LORD was over the tabernacle by day,
and fire was in the cloud by night ...' (v.38)

As we come to the conclusion of the Exodus story we find God present with His people in a powerful way. Earlier references to the cloud, the presence and the glory, have prepared us for this striking finale to the book. As the glory of the Lord fills the tabernacle Moses is unable to enter, just as, later, the priests would be unable to minister in the Temple when the glory cloud filled it (1 Kings 8:10).

Here we learn further wonderful things about God. We learn that God's holiness, His otherness, His majestic difference from us, does not indicate aloofness or distance from us. On the other hand, we learn that God's intimacy and nearness to us does not diminish His holiness or render Him tame and user-friendly. He remains the Holy One in our midst. We also learn that God is passionately determined to travel with His people, come what may, risking His own reputation, and becoming vulnerable in the process.

FURTHER STUDY

Heb. 13:10-15;
John 14:1-4;
Rev. 22:1-7

1. What are our altar and offerings?

2. What 'promised land' awaits the end of our journey?

As we leave this astonishing book let's do so with a heart full of gratitude that the God of Exodus is still the same today. He still hears the cry of His people, still saves and delivers, still speaks and stays true to His covenant, still guides and is present with us on our pilgrimage to the promised new creation.

The lasting image from the Exodus is of God's glory filling the tabernacle. Such glory must have been wonderful to behold for those who saw it. One day, however, the story of salvation was to be continued with the appearance of God's glory in the form of Jesus – Immanuel, God with us. And 'We have seen his glory' (John 1:14). What glory!

Gracious Father, I thank You that I have fellowship with a God who designed my freedom, delivers me from bondage, carries me through life's wilderness, and promises me He will never leave me. I can go on now, no matter what. Amen.

ORDER FORM

4 EASY WAYS TO ORDER:

1. Phone in your credit card order: **01252 784710** (Mon-Fri, 9.30am - 5pm)
2. Visit our Online Store at **www.cwr.org.uk/store**
3. Send this form together with your payment to:
   CWR, Waverley Abbey House, Waverley Lane, Farnham, Surrey GU9 8EP
4. Visit your local Christian bookshop

For a list of our National Distributors, who supply countries outside the UK, visit www.cwr.org.uk/distributors

YOUR DETAILS (REQUIRED FOR ORDERS AND DONATIONS)

Name: CWR ID No. (if known):

Home Address:

                                           Postcode:

Telephone No. (for queries):   Email:

PUBLICATIONS

TITLE	QTY	PRICE	TOTAL
		Total publications	

All CWR adult Bible-reading notes are also available in ebook and email subscription format.
Visit www.cwr.org.uk for further information.

UK p&p: up to £24.99 = **£2.99**; £25.00 and over = **FREE**

Elsewhere p&p: up to £10 = **£4.95**; £10.01 - £50 = **£6.95**; £50.01 - £99.99 = **£10**; £100 and over = **£30**

Please allow 14 days for delivery   Total publications and p&p **A**

SUBSCRIPTIONS* (NON DIRECT DEBIT)

SUBSCRIPTIONS* (NON DIRECT DEBIT)	QTY	PRICE (INCLUDING P&P)			TOTAL
		UK	Europe	Elsewhere	
Every Day with Jesus (1yr, 6 issues)		£15.95	£19.95	Please contact nearest National Distributor or CWR direct	
Large Print *Every Day with Jesus* (1yr, 6 issues)		£15.95	£19.95		
Inspiring Women Every Day (1yr, 6 issues)		£15.95	£19.95		
Life Every Day (Jeff Lucas) (1yr, 6 issues)		£15.95	£19.95		
Cover to Cover Every Day (1yr, 6 issues)		£15.95	£19.95		
Mettle: 14-18s (1yr, 3 issues)		£14.50	£16.60		
YP's: 11-15s (1yr, 6 issues)		£15.95	£19.95		
Topz: 7-11s (1yr, 6 issues)		£15.95	£19.95		
Total Subscriptions (Subscription prices already include postage and packing) **B**					

Please circle which bimonthly issue you would like your subscription to commence from:
Jan/Feb Mar/Apr May/Jun Jul/Aug Sep/Oct Nov/Dec

* Only use this section for subscriptions paid for by credit/debit card or cheque. For Direct Debit subscriptions see overleaf.

CONTINUED OVERLEAF >>

PAYMENT DETAILS

☐ I enclose a cheque/PO made payable to CWR for the amount of: £ _____

☐ Please charge my credit/debit card.

Cardholder's name (in BLOCK CAPITALS) _____

Card No. ☐☐☐☐ ☐☐☐☐ ☐☐☐☐ ☐☐☐☐

Expires end ☐☐☐☐   Security Code ☐☐☐

GIFT TO CWR   ☐ Please send me an acknowledgement of my gift   **C** ☐

GIFT AID (YOUR HOME ADDRESS REQUIRED, SEE OVERLEAF)

giftaid it

I am a UK taxpayer and want CWR to reclaim the tax on all my donations for the four years prior to this year **and on** all donations I make from the date of this Gift Aid declaration until further notice.*

Taxpayer's Full Name (in BLOCK CAPITALS) _____

Signature _____ **Date** _____

*I understand I must pay an amount of Income/Capital Gains Tax at least equal to the tax the charity reclaims in the tax year.

GRAND TOTAL (Total of A, B, & C) ☐

SUBSCRIPTIONS BY DIRECT DEBIT (UK BANK ACCOUNT HOLDERS ONLY)

Subscriptions cost £15.95 (except *Mettle*: £14.50) for one year for delivery within the UK. Please tick relevant boxes and fill in the form be

☐ *Every Day with Jesus* (1yr, 6 issues)
☐ Large Print *Every Day with Jesus* (1yr, 6 issues)
☐ *Inspiring Women Every Day* (1yr, 6 issues)
☐ *Life Every Day* (Jeff Lucas) (1yr, 6 issues)

☐ *Cover to Cover Every Day* (1yr, 6 issues)
☐ *Mettle*: 14-18s (1yr, 3 issues)
☐ *YP's*: 11-15s (1yr, 6 issues)
☐ *Topz*: 7-11s (1yr, 6 issues)

Issue to commence fr
☐ Jan/Feb ☐ Jul/Aug
☐ Mar/Apr ☐ Sep/Oct
☐ May/Jun ☐ Nov/Dec

CWR

Instruction to your Bank or Building Society to pay by Direct Debit

DIRECT Debit

Please fill in the form and send to: CWR, Waverley Abbey House, Waverley Lane, Farnham, Surrey GU9 8EP

Name and full postal address of your Bank or Building Society

To: The Manager _____ Bank/Building Society

Address _____

_____ Postcode _____

Name(s) of Account Holder(s)

_____

Branch Sort Code ☐☐ ☐☐ ☐☐

Bank/Building Society account number ☐☐☐☐☐☐☐☐

Originator's Identification Number

| 4 | 2 | 0 | 4 | 8 | 7 |

Reference

| | | | | | | | | | | | | | | | | | |

Instruction to your Bank or Building Society

Please pay CWR Direct Debits from the account detailed in this Instruction subj to the safeguards assured by the Direct Debit Guarantee.

I understand that this Instruction may remain with CWR and, if so, details will be passed electronically to my Bank/Building Society.

Signature(s)

_____

Date

Banks and Building Societies may not accept Direct Debit Instructions for some types of account